EDUCATION
FOR THE
HANDICAPPED CHILD
IN THE
ELEMENTARY CLASSROOM

Gary M. Clark
University of Kansas

LOVE PUBLISHING COMPANY
Denver · London

Copyright © 1979 Love Publishing Company
Printed in the U.S.A.
ISBN 0-89108-092-9
Library of Congress Catalog Card Number 78-78028
10 9 8 7 6 5 4 3 2 1

To Jeannie, Austin, and Amanda
. . . a very special family

PREFACE

Many books have been and will continue to be written on career education. Some might question the need for another one. It is my feeling that the current movement for a "free, appropriate education" for all handicapped children presents a challenge to the field of education in general and the career education movement in particular that demands some type of response to relate the two. Although the major themes of this book are the justification for, and planning and implementation of, career development instruction for all types of handicapped children, there is an underlying theme that speaks to the need of this type of instruction for *all* children.

Some advocates of career education focus primarily, if not entirely, on the development of occupational awareness, exploration, and preparation; I believe that is much too narrow a view, if "career" really refers to an individual's course or progress through life (as our dictionaries define the term). There is more to life than an occupational progression or a series of occupational experiences. There is more to education than preparation for occupations.

This book presents a model for deciding what curriculum content is appropriate for handicapped children and how it can be delivered in regular or special instructional programs. The material provides practical ideas for teachers, counselors, principals, curriculum coordinators, career education specialists, and special educators working at the elementary level. It also presents ideas for justifying, planning, and conducting the instruction so sorely needed by handicapped children — instruction to help them relate their personal, social, and occupational development to their life careers. I call this type of instruction "career education" because it is compatible with the theoretical assumptions of the career education movement, even though it takes a broader view than most current definitions.

The first chapter presents a relatively formal introduction to the concept of career education, including definitions, a rationale for career education programming, the basic career education models in current practice, and a proposed model for the handicapped. The remaining chapters are less formal, presenting a personal approach in a "how-to" format. Throughout, the material reflects my belief that the ideas are intended more as stimulus than as response, more as illustration than as final product.

If you work with or have some responsibility for any child with a physical, sensory, or mental impairment, this book should offer you a number of ideas and new perspectives on what career education instruction could mean to that child and how you, regardless of your role, can be an important participant in delivering that instruction.

I want to gratefully acknowledge the stimulation of ideas by such leaders in the field as Dr. Kenneth B. Hoyt, Dr. Rupert N. Evans, Dr. Donn E. Brolin, Dr. Norman Gysbers, and Dr. S. P. Marland. I am especially appreciative of the open exchange with my students at the University of Kansas where this model and these ideas evolved. Their interest, enthusiasm, and tolerance kept me on task. I also want to acknowledge Mina Carr and Sue Elkins, who provided excellent practical support by typing and editing the manuscript, and the University of Kansas, which granted me a sabbatical that gave me time to complete this book.

Gary M. Clark

CONTENTS

1

CAREER EDUCATION FOR THE HANDICAPPED: WHAT, WHY, AND HOW

If there were ever a movement in education that could be described as a curriculum movement, career education is certainly one. It is directed at specific changes in our schools' curricular *content* and *level of instruction* and it is having a definite impact on educational theory and practice. Whether one sees it as just another movement in education, a passing fad, or a reflex action to sudden pressures on the American education system, career education must be acknowledged as an increasingly potent force in education today. Its proponents are following the lead of former U.S. Commissioner of Education, Sidney P. Marland, Jr., and Associate Commissioner for Career Education, Kenneth B. Hoyt. Interest is spurred on by public statements or endorsements by various members of Congress, the National Association of Secondary School Officers, the U.S. Chamber of Commerce, and with some qualifications, the educational leadership of AFL-CIO. Congress provided support by passing The Elementary and Secondary Career Education Act of 1977 to further encourage leadership for career education.

1

Over the past five or six years many educators have come to view career education as a focus around which all education can be developed. This is especially true of educators of the handicapped, who have long advocated the basic principles of career education, while also seeing it as a desirable change within the mainstream of education that would permit greater accommodation of the handicapped.

Since many of the concepts of career education have already been advocated for the handicapped in public schools (DeProspo and Hungerford, 1946; Hungerford, 1941; Kirk and Johnson, 1951; Kolstoe, 1970; Martens, 1937), you might ask why educators of handicapped elementary school children should be drawn into the movement of career education, especially when it appears so similar to current emphases in secondary special education. There are several reasons. First, some basic concepts of career education must be started early, years before the secondary level. Second, the emphasis in career education at the elementary level is *not* the same as at the secondary level; there should be no conflict between the two programs. Finally, if career education is going to survive as a movement, the elementary school curriculum and elementary school professionals must lead the movement and provide direction.

With this in mind, let us attempt to clarify the scope and sequence of career education and examine its vital relevance to education of the handicapped in the elementary school. We will need to define career education and its rationale, delineate its goals, and describe current conceptualizations of its evolving structure. We will then look at a model for career education for the handicapped with emphasis on its implications for appropriate education of young handicapped children.

WHAT IS CAREER EDUCATION?

There is no universally endorsed definition of career education. It is hoped that this lack of definition will encourage divergent groups to explore the problem and contribute to the overall body of knowledge, from which a truly meaningful definition could emerge. Such a definition would, in essence, be a descriptive statement of the concept after it had been studied, debated, applied, analyzed, and evaluated, rather than a forced definition that would prestructure all study, debate, application, analysis, and evaluation of the concept.

Hoyt (Budke, Bettis, and Beasley, 1972) was one of the first to attempt a formal definition after career education was launched as a movement in 1971. His definition was as follows:

> Career education represents the total effort of public education and the community to help all individuals become familiar with the values of a work oriented society, to integrate those values into their personal value structure, and to implement those values in their lives in ways that make work possible, meaningful; and satisfying to each individual. (p. 3)

Hoyt (General Learning Corporation, 1972) later qualified this definition by pointing out that there is an inherent assumption that "work values" encompass a variety of motivations, including, though not limited to, the classical Protestant work ethic. This is important, because if we were to interpret the definition solely in terms of the traditional Protestant work ethic, it opens an avenue of argument against the general validity of the concept of career education.

Gordon (1973) raises the question of the importance of work in personal fulfillment with his observation that work may no longer be central in the new social order. As radical as this may sound, we only have to observe the mass media's emphasis on leisure activities as the central focus of our lives to see some support for the notion.

Although it is true that there is no universal definition of career education, the U.S. Office of Education (Hoyt, 1975) presented a definition in a policy paper on career education that has been widely accepted and used as a basis for programming. Since Associate Commissioner of Education Kenneth B. Hoyt authored the paper, the definition shows only a slight change in emphasis from the 1972 definition. The policy definition is as follows:

> Career education is the totality of experiences through which one learns about and prepares to engage in work as part of her or his way of living. (p. 4)

3

The definition is based on Hoyt's interpretation of "career" and "education." He considers "career" to be the totality of work one does in his or her lifetime (beginning in the very early years and continuing through the retirement years) and "education" to be the totality of experiences through which one learns (including far more than formal education). This generic definition is purposely intended to be of a broad and encompassing nature but, at the same time, it is also intended to encompass considerably less than all of life or a sole reason for living.

The significant difference between Hoyt's 1972 and 1975 definitions is the shift of emphasis from "values of a work oriented society" to "experiences through which one learns about and prepares to engage in work." The new emphasis on "work" resulted in a need for clarification of what is meant by the term. Hoyt (no date) defined work this way:

> "Work" is conscious effort aimed at producing benefits for oneself and/or for oneself and others. As such, it is unimportant whether such effort is paid or unpaid in nature. What is important is that it represents the basic need of all human beings to achieve — to accomplish — to *do* something productive that allows the individual to discover both who he/she is and why he/she is. With this definition, work is properly viewed as a human right — not a societal obligation. (p. 2)

Hoyt (1975) is even more specific in another statement:

> "Work" is conscious effort, other than that involved in activities whose primary purpose is either coping or relaxing, aimed at producing benefits for oneself and/or for oneself and others. (p. 3)

These definitions make no distinction between the work of the musician, the athlete, the salesman, the bricklayer, the homemaker, the lawyer, or the do-it-yourself homeowner. Some work requires intensive coaching and personal preparation; other work may require learning on the job or, perhaps, an advanced degree. In most (if not all) cases, however, being "successful" typically requires some learned set of job or daily living skills.

How do these definitions affect the handicapped child? First, there is the implication that work for the handicapped child can be a part of his or her way of living and that he or she can make a conscious effort while growing up to learn about and prepare for some kind of beneficial productivity (work) in the here-and-now as well as in the future. Work does not have to be paid employment or something that one does as an adult. Work is also possible for children.

A second implication is that although work itself, rather than the "values of a work oriented society," is increasingly being accepted as the focus of career education, both definitions assume that a handicapped child must learn about the *right* to work long before paid employment enters the picture. The child also needs to learn that if *satisfying* paid employment does not occur, it is not necessarily because of his or her handicap per se. It is more likely that factors outside of the handicapping condition, such as societal attitudes, the occupational counseling and placement skills of professionals who will advise them, or the effects of recession or depression on the economy, will affect their job satisfaction. The definitions encourage all people to consider themselves acceptable human beings whether or not they are paid workers and whether or not their work brings them personal fulfillment. For too long we have made people feel guilty for not being able to use their vocations as "identity realization" or "self-actualizing" opportunities. Work occurring in paid employment may be only a means to one of several ends — survival, safety or security, belonging or love, esteem, self-actualization (Maslow, 1954). Work in unpaid situations may be just as conducive to personal fulfillment or self-actualization as work in a paid vocation.

These interpretations of implications for the handicapped are probably as valid as any, but there is no doubt that the underlying theme of Hoyt's definitions reflects a definite bias toward a person's economic life (paid work). The definitions and their elaborations also attempt to restore the credibility of the Protestant work ethic by emphasizing the positive aspects of work and reordering work ethic values, which have shifted over the years or been changed through distorted applications.

Not all definitions of career education accept this emphasis on the work ethic. Some professionals argue that we must go beyond work activities and work roles and learn about and prepare for other roles, settings, and events in a person's life. Gordon (1973, p. 59) proposes that the meaning of "career" is best understood when defined as "the course by which one develops and lives a responsible and satisfying life." This definition suggests that career education should be a series of experiences to provide knowledge for a person's life span, including possible roles as learner, producer, consumer, citizen, family member, and social-political being. In a more personal way, this conceptualization is echoed by Larry Allen, a 1972 high school graduate of Searcy, Arkansas. He stated:

> I hope that when the time comes to follow a Career Education plan in public schools we don't limit the concept implied by the term "Career Education." In the future, the work careers of Americans will constitute only a portion of our daily lives. . . . To lead full, useful lives, on the job and off, we must be prepared to develop ourselves into well-rounded individuals. (Allen, 1973, p. 162)

Goldhammer (1972) is another advocate of this point of view and he defines career education in the context of a "careers curriculum." Such a curriculum would be based on the various life careers individuals experience as participants in society: producers of goods or renderers of services; members of family groups; participants in social and political activities; participants in avocational pursuits; and participants in functions involving aesthetic, religious, and moral concerns. Nash and Agne (1973) and Spradley (1973) also support this broader perspective on career education.

Gysbers and Moore (1974) propose a similar approach in their educational-guidance model for "life career development." Life career development is defined as "self development over the life span through the integration of the roles, settings, and events of a person's total life" (p. 10). Cross (1974) has taken a parallel position in his "careers" education model for the elementary level. He suggests that if life is to be a fulfilling experience, individuals must experience a degree of success in *all* aspects of living. He proposes that elementary education should be organized around the life careers that have the greatest influence on living in America — career as a family member, career as a citizen, career as a member of a vocation, and career as a pursuer of avocational interests.

Clark (1974) and Brolin (1974) see career education for the handicapped as having an equally broad scope, going beyond occupational awareness, exploration, and preparation. Clark, referring to Gordon's (1973) definition of career cited above, states that career education

> concerns itself with a merging of liberal education and vocational development such that it facilitates the *process of living* and is not limited to facilitating the *process of making* a living. (p. 10)

Brolin has outlined a series of twenty-two competencies that he believes to be essential for the educable mentally retarded; a useful career education curriculum should be developed around these objectives. Work and occupational development comprise only one of three major areas he uses in organizing his competencies. The major curriculum areas include daily living skills, occupational guidance and preparation, and personal-social skills. He defines career education as "systematically coordinating all school, family, and community components together to facilitate each individual's potential for economic, social, and personal fulfillment" (Brolin, 1974, p. 5).

What are the implications of these definitions for the handicapped child? They obviously reflect concern for more aspects of life career development than work. They provide a strong argument for expending significant educational effort on teaching skills for current and future adjustment needs as a person, a social being, and a citizen, as well as a productive worker. The important point for the elementary level professional, in terms of the needs of the handicapped, is that career education must not be judged on the basis of any one definition, but rather be evaluated from all the definitions. Understanding what its primary purposes might include requires an open mind; the definitions must be taken as idealistic statements of intent.

7

Career education is not yet a static, definable notion, in spite of the efforts of local, state, and federal educators to "pin it down" through official statements. There is still substantial disagreement among individuals and groups, but the differences may not be as great as they seem.

There is reason to believe that some public education officials assume a strong position on work as the basic theme of career education because of the political realities of the times. They are sensitive to the fact that Congress, state legislatures, and local school boards are much more responsive to educational programs that address current problems in unemployment, economic recession, work alienation, and welfare support than to programs emphasizing life roles or life careers. Fortunately, most teachers, counselors, and administrators do not have to deal directly with the political complexities surrounding career education. Nonetheless, an understanding of the issues involved can be useful when attempting to develop teaching or guidance strategies. The knowledge is certainly valuable to educators faced with a parent who asks, "What is this career education?"

WHY CAREER EDUCATION?

A parent's next question may well be, "Why do we need a special program for that? Isn't that what schools are supposed to have been doing all these years?" The response has to be based on an acknowledgement of our educational failures in the past. There is no doubt that career education is only one of several possible responses that could be made to the demand for educational reform.

According to Hoyt (1975), career education is an attempt to correct the following criticisms of American education:

1. Too many persons leaving our educational system are deficient in the basic academic skills required for adaptability in today's rapidly changing society.
2. Too many students fail to see meaningful relationships between what they are being asked to learn in

school and what they will do when they leave the educational system. This is true of those who remain to graduate as well as those who drop out of the educational system.

3. American education as currently structured best meets the educational needs of the minority — those who will someday become college graduates. It fails to place equal emphasis on meeting the educational needs of the vast majority of students who will never be college graduates.

4. American education has not kept pace with change in the post-industrial occupational society. As a result, when worker qualifications are compared with job requirements, we find overeducated and undereducated workers present in large numbers. The boredom of the overeducated worker and the frustration of the under-educated worker have contributed to growing worker alienation in the total occupational society.

5. Too many persons leave our educational system at the secondary and collegiate levels unequipped with appropriate vocational skills, self-understanding and career decision-making skills, or work attitudes essential for making a successful transition from school to work.

6. The growing need for women in the work force has not been reflected adequately in the educational or career options typically presented to girls enrolled in our educational system.

7. The growing needs for continuing and recurrent education for adults are not being adequately met by our current systems of public education.

8. Insufficient attention has been given to learning opportunities outside the structure of formal education, when they are increasingly needed by both youth and adults in our society.

9. The general public (including parents and the business-industry-labor community) has not been given an adequate role in formulation of educational policy.

10. As currently structured, American education does not adequately meet the needs of minority or economically disadvantaged persons in our society.
11. Post-high school education has given insufficient emphasis to educational programs at the sub-baccalaureate degree level (p. 1-2).

If statistics make these criticisms any more believable, the following figures appear frequently in career education rationale statements:

—In 1970-71 close to 2.5 million students left the formal education system of the United States without adequate preparation for careers. Of these, 850,000 were dropouts from elementary and secondary schools; 750,000 were general high school graduates who did not enter any post-secondary training and had no marketable skill; 850,000 were dropouts from college or other post-secondary programs (Marland, 1971).

—For the 1980s it is predicted that 80 percent of all job openings will require less than a college education (Russo, 1972).

—The average person must go back to school or receive some kind of training or retraining seven to nine times in his or her lifetime (Russo, 1972).

—The Bureau of the Census lists 250 different occupations, but half of all working women are employed in only 21 of them, usually the low-pay, low-responsibility jobs. (Sheehy, 1977).

—General education enrolls 25 percent of those who graduate from high school, *but* it produces about 70 percent of all high school dropouts; it produced about 88 percent of all Manpower and Development Act trainees when that governmental training was available; and it produces at least 78 percent of the inmates of correctional institutions (Pucil, 1968).

Barone (1973) made the following predictions regarding the

approximately 2.5 million handicapped youth who he estimated would leave our school systems during 1973-77:

—525,000 (21 percent) will be either fully employed or enrolled in college.
—1,000,000 (40 percent) will be *underemployed* and at the poverty level.
—200,000 (8 percent) will be in their home community and idle much of the time.
—650,000 (26 percent) will be *unemployed* and on welfare.
—75,000 (3 percent) will be totally dependent and institutionalized.

Predictions such as these, if anywhere near accurate, are disconcerting, if not devastating. What greater indictment could be made of a special education system and society? What sort of system permits almost 80 percent of our handicapped youth to be less than fully employed at a reasonable wage and blocks involvement in further education?

The "why" of career education relative to work becomes obvious, given the data presented above. If similar data were available on our "success" rate with the handicapped as consumers, family members, and citizens, we might be even more alarmed at our educational shortcomings. Criticisms of our educational programs from former students, parents, and the business-industrial community, dropouts, minority groups, and the general public make the need for change in the system unquestionable. Many see career education as the creative answer for a positive reform movement.

HOW CAN CAREER EDUCATION BE PLANNED AND IMPLEMENTED?

Planning a career education program for handicapped children at the elementary level must be based on goals and objectives specifically set for them. In order to establish what goals and objectives should be set, some basic assumptions

11

must first be considered. The ones suggested here are based on a series of assumptions presented in the U.S. Office of Education policy paper, *An Introduction to Career Education* (Hoyt, 1975):

1. Career education is for all persons — young and old, gifted and retarded, visually handicapped and sighted, male and female, poor and affluent — all races, and all ethnic groups.

2. A career, like an education, is a developmental process and should be viewed from that planning perspective.

3. The nature of our society demands that career education espouse a multiplicity of work values rather than a single work ethic so that children can formulate their own answer to the question, "Why should I work?"

4. A continuing concern of career education is protecting each child's freedom to make choices and decisions while teaching him or her what the alternatives are.

5. Significant deprivation in any aspect of human growth can affect career development. Children who have experienced deprivation will require special variation or individualization in career development programs.

6. There are a number of historical and current limitations imposed by society upon the life career development of handicapped persons. They include stereotyping, negative attitudes, architectural barriers, and limitations in goal selection and decision-making. These, limitations make career development more complex and time consuming for many handicapped persons.

7. Any person choosing to work in today's complex and rapidly changing work world must possess adaptable skills. Adaptability stems from a strong foundation in basic academic skills, a personally meaningful set of work values, positive human relationships, good work habits, knowledge of occupational alternatives, an understanding of the nature and realities of the world of work, and some actual job skills.

Career Education Goals for the Handicapped

The goals for elementary level handicapped children presented here reflect my position on the ideal conceptualization of career education and the general scope of programming that should occur at the elementary level (K-6). From that perspective, career education should be designed and implemented to:

—provide instruction and guidance for developing positive habits, attitudes, and values toward work and daily living;
—provide instruction and guidance for establishing and maintaining positive human relationships at home, school, and at work;
—provide instruction and guidance for developing awareness of occupational alternatives;
—provide instruction for an orientation to the realities of the world of work, as a producer and as a consumer;
—provide instruction for acquisition of actual job and daily living skills.

These goals not only emphasize work as a significant part of life careers, but also provide for the mutually important aspects of life careers in the personal and social areas. Each of these goals will be elaborated upon in the following chapters.

Career Education: A Proposed Structure

The U.S. Office of Education has formulated four models of career education or, rather, four alternative ways of facilitating career education goals. Substantial efforts are being made to support research and development of career education through the National Center for Educational Research and Development by concentrating resources on these four models or delivery systems:

1. The employer-based model;
2. The home/community-based model;

3. The residential-based model; and
4. The school-based model.

Each model can provide handicapped youth and adults with some of the advantages of career education. Since many educators of the handicapped may be familiar only with the school-based model, we will briefly describe all four models to establish a perspective for the complete proposed structure and scope of career education.

Employer-Based Career Education Model

This model is being developed, operated, and supported primarily by business and industry in cooperation with school systems. The target population is the thirteen to twenty age group and, as might be expected in an out-of-school program, many of the target individuals are characterized as "unmotivated, alienated, and disaffected." However, the model is intended to be a legitimate, viable option for any student. Its primary goal is to provide a comprehensive set of personalized educational experiences for junior or senior high school students who *voluntarily* choose this approach to education over the traditional classroom approach.

Two key elements of this model include defining individual learning needs and locating actual work situations in which those needs can be met. A special attempt is made to allow each student to participate in defining those needs and selecting the work situation from a variety of opportunities. The model provides for the completion of high school graduation requirements.

Budke, Bettis, and Beasley (1972) report that employer-based career education projects are planned to be developed and operated by consortia of business and other public or private organizations. These consortia are being sponsored by selected agencies across the country under contract to the U.S. Office of Education to develop and field test the model. Some of these agencies include Research for Better Schools, Inc.

(Philadelphia); the Far West Laboratory for Educational Research and Development (Berkeley, California); the Northwest Regional Educational Laboratory (Portland, Oregon); and the Appalachia Educational Laboratory (Charleston, West Virginia).

Home/Community-Based Career Education Model

The home-based model is designed to reach individuals who have left the traditional school environment but who need or desire further education. The population for which this model is designed ranges in age from eighteen to twenty-five and includes those who spend most of their time at home, such as pregnant women or mothers of preschool children, unemployed persons, or handicapped persons with short-term or relatively permanent disabling conditions.

The delivery of this model can take several approaches. One follows a mass media approach that emphasizes motivating individuals to study for career development. Television and radio are the media that would be most frequently used. Another approach involves direct instruction to individuals at home via cable television, correspondence programs, telephone hook-ups, audio cassettes, radio, and instructional kits designed for specific content areas. A third, supplementary approach is the establishment of career clinics in community or neighborhood centers to provide personal career guidance and counseling, referral services, and information on relevant career-oriented education programs that are or will be available.

Rural Residential Career Education Model

A typical criticism of many new education and training programs is that the only people who can benefit from them are those who live in or near urban areas. The rural residential model is proposed as a partial solution to this problem and offers what is perhaps the boldest, most imaginative model for the delivery of career education opportunities.

15

It is presently designed to serve isolated, disadvantaged families or unmarried individuals from a geographical region covering no more than six states. It attempts to provide rural residents with the development and improvement of employment capabilities appropriate to their area. The program should stimulate economic development of the area by introducing new occupational possibilities and providing training for them, as well as improving family life in general.

At this point, the model is a research and demonstration project testing the hypothesis that entire families from disadvantaged or isolated areas can improve their economic and social situations through an intensive program at a residential center. This involves moving individuals and families from their home environments to a setting designed to provide a comprehensive array of services including day care, kindergarten, elementary and secondary education, career and technical education, adult education, parent/family assistance, medical and dental services, welfare services, counseling and guidance, and cultural and recreational opportunities for both single and married participants and their families.

School-Based Career Education Model

The school-based model for career education is being developed through a grant to the Center for Vocational and Technical Education at The Ohio State University in Columbus, Ohio. Marland (1971) has presented one version of this model (see Figure 1.1), which depicts the vertical and horizontal progression of career education as a pyramid that begins with "career awareness" in the elementary grades and moves to a specific orientation to the work world as the student progresses through school.

Marland's version of the model appears to center on an occupational guidance and skill acquisition program. A major criticism thus far of career education as a movement has been the difficulty of differentiating between vocational education and career education. The traditional concepts of the goals of

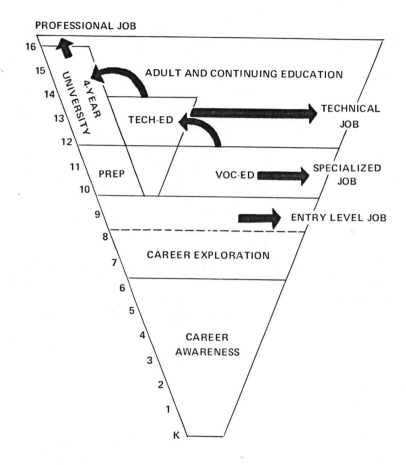

Figure 1.1. Marland's school-based career education model.

vocational and technical education are so enmeshed in Marland's model that parents, teachers, academicians, and students lose sight of the scope of career education objectives.

Figure 1.2 clarifies how each of the models relates to vocational education. Clearly, vocational education is only a small part of career education, although Marland's (1971) model and its subsequent variations have taken the position that work, in the traditional sense of paid employment, is the

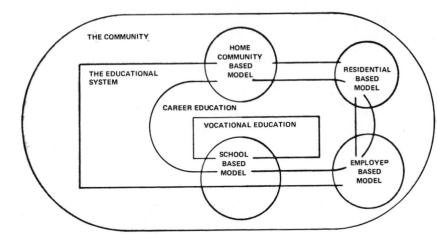

Figure 1.2. Relationship of models to vocational education.

basic theme and little emphasis has been placed on other life career roles.

The school-based model attempts to create a comprehensive awareness of job options while increasing a student's ability to enter employment in a selected occupational area or go on for further education. But the model also seeks to develop a concept of self in relation to work, personal characteristics (like initiative, resourcefulness, and pride in work), and a realistic understanding of the relationships between the world of work and education. The emphasis the model places on career awareness, career exploration, and entry-level job skill acquisition reflects the most central thrust of the movement, but it may also cause undue criticism of the concept of career education. Regardless of this emphasis, there is no doubt that Marland (1971), Hoyt (1975), and other supporters of the model view career education as a unique program whose ultimate outcome is a satisfied and satisfying worker in our society.

Figure 1.3 shows a school-based model for the handicapped that reflects my own orientation. This model maintains a focus on work careers, but gives equal importance to other competencies critical to life careers and involves roles in addition to

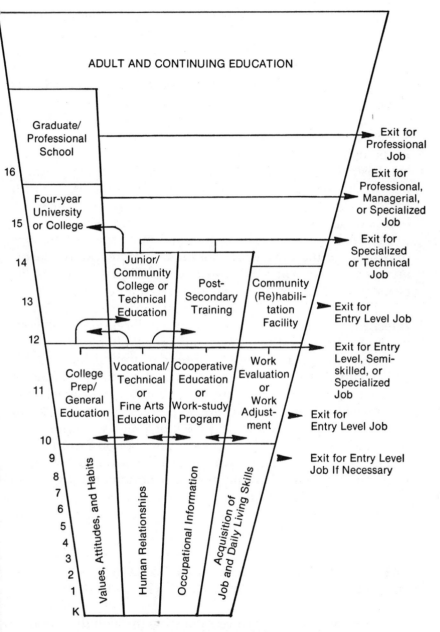

Figure 1.3. A school-based career education model for the handicapped.

worker roles. The curricula of the elementary school (K-6) and junior high school (7-9) would both be based around the mutually important elements of (a) attitudes, values, and habits; (b) human relationships; (c) occupational information; and (d) acquisition of job and daily living skills. These four elements change in their nature as pupils progress through the grade hierarchy and as the sequence of objectives is accomplished. An example of this is the change in the nature of objectives in occupational information. The objectives in grades K-6 emphasize occupational roles, occupational vocabulary, awareness of occupational alternatives, and general familiarity with some of the realities of the world of work. In grades 7-9, occupational exploration, initial matching of job requirements to personal interests and abilities, and more specific coverage of realities of the work world are stressed. More specific elaboration of the content and sequencing of objectives across the elementary grades will be made in succeeding chapters.

The vertical lines dividing the four major components of career education at the elementary and junior high school levels are meant to suggest that these components should actually be extended through adult and continuing education. The graphic placement of advanced preparation and training options in relation to the components of career education in grades K-9 is coincidental and should not be perceived as a "track" or progression. There *is* a logical track or progression, however, for entering and pursuing preparation options from grade 10 on up. Even there, the arrows reflect the possibility of movement among the options, negating any notion of being locked in. Variations do not imply simple exchanges; a preparation option's prerequisites and requirements would still need to be met.

IMPLICATIONS OF CAREER EDUCATION
FOR THE ELEMENTARY HANDICAPPED CHILD

The implications of career education through the proposed school-based model for mentally and physically handicapped individuals depend somewhat on the success of the movement within general education. As a concept, it affirms the proposals for personal, social, prevocational, and vocational training for the handicapped that have existed for some time. However, as a movement, it will have varying degrees of impact on the handicapped as a group, depending upon the extent of its implementation.

Most current efforts at career education development at the state and local levels appear to be concentrating on general programming and implementation procedures for regular education programs. There is general agreement that these programming efforts have been more widely accepted in regular education by elementary teachers than by secondary teachers. This is extremely advantageous for elementary handicapped children, since they may consequently receive as much or more career education programming through their regular class instruction than in a special self-contained class or learning center. Special program options for handicapped children, particularly those for the learning disabled, emotionally disturbed, and mildly retarded, are still emphasizing cognitive development and academic remediation; they generally give inadequate attention to the scope of career education advocated here.

The most obvious disability groups that would benefit from a broad school-based career education model are the mildly retarded and the learning disabled. Since these two groups are the largest within the public schools, they are likely to be worked into general career education programs of some kind. However, Budke, Bettis, and Beasley (1972) reviewed twenty-six career education programs in twenty-two states and found that only one-third (nine) claimed to have any special instruction for handicapped youth in career education and less than 10 percent of the twenty-six programs provided a component for the educable retarded. It is not clear whether these figures reflect a lack of special education programs in career education programming or whether the mildly handicapped in public schools are becoming "invisible" to the extent that they are included in regular programs without special labels. No recent studies show any improvements in this situation.

The school-based model emphasizes a sequential approach

21

to career education that includes the partially sighted, hard of hearing, mildly developmentally disabled, and orthopedically handicapped. Programs for these individuals should feel the impact of what is being taught in the regular grades at the elementary and junior high school levels and there should be some curricular revisions in self-contained classes or learning/resource centers to ensure that students are receiving a comparable foundation in career preparation.

The goals of "career awareness leading to career identity" and "self-awareness leading to self-identity" developed for the school-based model by the Center for Vocational and Technical Education at The Ohio State University (Budke, Bettis, and Beasley, 1972, p. 10) are vital to career development for the handicapped. They are especially crucial in the level of employment the handicapped will eventually attain. Occupational identity and self-identity are demonstrated in what individuals allow themselves to be guided into by parents, teachers, counselors, friends, or circumstances. Handicapped persons have enough problems dealing with stereotyped ideas of occupational and personal identity on the part of the nonhandicapped. The implications of this model for the long-term pursuit of these two goals by the handicapped are exciting when contrasted to what has been provided in the past.

SUMMARY

Career education, as a concept, is rapidly evolving into a movement with structure and definable parameters. It is still misunderstood by some as to its intent, its scope, and its structure, but increasingly more information is being made available to educators and the general public to respond to these misconceptions. As it evolves into what is to be, there need to be continuous reminders of what it is *not*.

— Career education is *not* vocational education with a new name.
— Career education is *not* a new educational movement to replace or downgrade academic education.

— Career education is *not* a system bound to traditional school ages.
— Career education is *not* a program to be limited to any one environment.
— Career education is *not* training for a single occupation.
— Career education is *not* a program for one educational population.

Handicapped children fit into the schema of career education as readily as any group and stand to gain from its offerings. Further, it is critical that such programming be provided. Those interested in the welfare of the handicapped, however, must move aggressively into the arena of career education development if there is to be a significant impact from the movement on the careers of the handicapped. Career education curricula must give equal consideration to the mutually important aspects of career development: attitudes, values, and habits; human relationships; occupational information; and acquisition of job and daily living skills.

REFERENCES

Allen, L. A 1972 high school graduate looks at career education. In L. McClure and C. Buan (eds.), *Essays on career education*. Portland, Oregon: Northwest Regional Educational Laboratory, 1973.

Barone, C. S. Paper presented to a Forum of National Organizations sponsored by the Vocational Evaluation and Work Adjustment Association, the National Rehabilitation Association, and the President's Committee for the Employment of the Handicapped, October 25, 1973.

Brolin, D. E. *Programming retarded in career education*. Working paper No. 1, Project PRICE, Department of Counseling and Personnel Services, University of Missouri-Columbia, 1974.

Budke, W. E., Bettis, G. E., and Beasley, G. F. *Career education practice*. Columbus, Ohio: ERIC Clearinghouse on Vocational and Technical Education, December, 1972.

Clark, G. M. Career education for the mildly handicapped. *Focus on Exceptional Children* 5 (9) (1974): 1-10.

Cross, F. R. *Elementary school careers education: A humanistic model*. Columbus, Ohio: Charles E. Merrill, 1974.

DeProspo, C. J., and Hungerford, R. H. A complete social program for the mentally retarded. *American Journal of Mental Deficiency* 51 (1946): 115-122.

General Learning Corporation. *Career education resource guide.* Morristown, New Jersey: General Learning Corporation, 1972.

Goldhammer, K. A careers curriculum. In K. Goldhammer and R. E. Taylor (eds.), *Career education: Perspective and promise.* Columbus, Ohio: Charles E. Merrill, 1972.

Gordon, E. W. Broadening the concept of career education. In L. McClure and C. Buan (eds.), *Essays on career education.* Portland, Oregon: Northwest Regional Educational Laboratory, 1973.

Gysbers, N. C., and Moore, E. J. *Career guidance, counseling and placement elements of an illustrative program guide.* University of Missouri-Columbia: Career Guidance, Counseling and Placement Project, 1974.

Hoyt, K. B. *An introduction to career education.*Policy paper of the U.S. Office of Education, DHEW Publications No. (OE) 75-00504, Washington, D.C.: U.S. Government Printing Office, 1975.

_____. *Career education and the handicapped person.* Unpublished address. U.S. Office of Education, Washington, D.C., no date.

Hungerford, R. H. The Detroit plan for the occupational education of the mentally retarded. *American Journal of Mental Deficiency* 46 (1941): 102-108.

Kirk, S. A., and Johnson, G. O. *Educating the retarded child.* Cambridge, Massachusetts: Riverside Press, 1951.

Kolstoe, O. P. *Teaching educable mentally retarded children.* New York: Holt, Rinehart, & Winston, 1970.

Marland, S. P., Jr. *Career education now.* Speech presented to the Convention of the National Association of Secondary School Principals in Houston, Texas, January 23, 1971.

Martens, E. H. Occupational preparation for mentally handicapped children. *Proceedings and Addresses of the Sixty-first Annual Session of the American Association on Mental Deficiency* 42 (1937): 157-165.

Maslow, A. H. *Motivation and personality.* New York: Harper and Row, 1954.

Nash, R. J., and Agne, R. M. Career education: Earning a living or living a life. *Phi Delta Kappan* 54 (1973): 373-378.

Pucil, D. J. Variables related to MDTA trainee success in Minnesota. Unpublished manuscript, University of Minnesota, 1968.

Russo, M. Speech presented to Governor's Conference on Career Education, Manhattan, Kansas, 1972.

Sheehy, G. *Passages.* New York: Bantam Books, 1977.

Spradley, J. P. Career education in cultural perspective. In L. McClure and C. Buan (eds.), *Essays on career education.* Portland, Oregon: Northwest Regional Educational Laboratory, 1973.

2

CAREER EDUCATION PROGRAMMING FOR VALUES, ATTITUDES, AND HABITS

When values, attitudes, and habits are cited as relevant curriculum areas of today's schools, many agree wholeheartedly, others hedge and raise qualifying aspects, and some actively oppose such a position. Parents and educators are to be found supporting each of these viewpoints; they do so because of their *own* values, attitudes, and habits.

One of the main reasons for concern about schools becoming involved in the process of developing and fostering values, attitudes, and habits is the problem of determining *which* values, attitudes, and habits should be taught. Values, for example, can be associated with any number of things — money, religious beliefs, race, education, sex, responsibility, integrity, loyalty to country, work, leisure — and many of them are controversial and sensitive issues.

Some people believe the schools should respond to the need for establishing and maintaining value systems that are positive for both the students and the social groups to which they belong. But what is a positive value system and, even if it can be identified, what do the schools do if there is a conflict between that value system and another held by someone from a different social group? The courts must continually provide legal answers to such questions — like teaching the theory of evolution, prayer in the schools, or the length of a person's hair or hemline — but the issues remain largely unresolved in the minds of thousands of individuals.

There is no doubt that our nation has historically maintained a sense of national identity on certain basic values, but the pluralistic approach to our democratic form of government has also forced us into accepting a multiple-value system much different from the single-value system that we have idealized. This discrepancy between the actual and the ideal has led to internal conflicts and a continuing state of confrontation, challenge, questioning, and social resolution.

Raths, Merrill, and Sidney (1966) have offered us a workable compromise, if not a solution, to the "teach values — do not teach values" dilemma by suggesting that educators should be concerned not with the *content* of people's values, but with the *process* of valuing. According to Raths et al., the valuing process consists of seven subprocesses, including the following:

Prizing one's beliefs and behaviors
1. Prizing and cherishing
2. Publicly affirming, when appropriate

Choosing one's beliefs and behaviors
3. Choosing from alternatives
4. Choosing after consideration of consequences
5. Choosing freely

Acting on one's beliefs
6. Acting
7. Acting with a pattern, consistency, and repetition.

This approach changes the focus from teaching children certain value-laden concepts to teaching children to select, defend, and act in those concept areas with an understanding of *why* they think or believe as they do, *how* their actions are related to those beliefs, and *what* the probable consequences of their actions will be.

Unfortunately, those who believe the schools should maintain and preserve certain moral and social values are not always willing to accept compromises. To them, any solution that completely avoids value content begs the question. It is my belief that the valuing process is of great importance in career education for the handicapped and it should be central to elementary level programming in this area. However, the valuing process should not be taught to the exclusion of other critical content areas, such as *work* (as defined by Hoyt, 1975b), *leisure, personal responsibility, learning,* and *equal opportunity.*

Thus far we have not introduced a rationale specifically geared toward attitudes or habits. The reason is that values, attitudes, and habits are considered to be so interdependent that a rationale for one is a rationale for the other two. Values — beliefs that are cherished — lead persons to assume attitudes or positions that reflect those beliefs. These attitudes, in turn, are manifested in relatively consistent, predictable behaviors or habits.

Further rationale for the importance of programming for values, attitudes, and habits goes beyond an educational philosophy. Butler and Browning (1974), Cobb (1972), Goldstein (1964), and Henrich and Kriegel (1961) have concluded from the literature on adult adjustment of the handicapped and personal reports of handicapped persons that these human variables are of critical importance. In most cases, they seem to be more important to the handicapped than actual job skills in maintaining employment and successfully fulfilling roles in the home and community. The research of Stephens (1972) strongly suggests that moral judgment (based on values) and moral conduct (attitudes and habits) in children of normal and below average intelligence are developmental traits and, as such, can be changed through education and training.

The quotations included below from handicapped and non-handicapped people recount life career experiences that reflect values, attitudes, or habits. They give subjective testimony in support of the need for some attention to valuing, attitudes, and habits in career development education.

Leonard Kriegel

As soon as I could get out of bed, I began to exercise — push-ups, sit-ups, lifting weights . . . I must also confess to a warm pride that floods my very being whenever I think back to those days . . . All that I wanted was to protect the growing self that I felt within me. . . .

I allowed nothing, no one, to violate that embryo of selfhood. I remember one time, lying in a pool of sweat on the linoleum-covered floor of my bedroom, when my mother entered my room, begging me in a tearful, frightened voice to come into the kitchen for dinner. I told her to get out, with all the anger I could muster against a threat to my new existence. And then I continued my push-ups, the ache in my shoulders growing almost as quickly as the pride in my mind, until I collapsed on the floor, gasping for breath, the salt taste of my own sweat running into my mouth. And for the first time in my life, I knew what was meant by pride in oneself. (Henrich & Kriegel, 1961, pp. 58-59)

John DeWitt McKee

When Will Shakespeare murmurs in my inner ear, "Sweet are the uses of adversity," my inner voice is likely to retort, "Speak for yourself, Will." There is nothing sweet about being past forty and still doing exercises in physical therapy to improve my balance and to correct a gait that has more than once been ascribed to drunkenness. There is nothing sweet in feeling good about the gait and suddenly catching sight of my lurching reflection in the window of a store or seeing my shadow bobbing grotesquely before me. Still, if the uses of adversity are not sweet, they *are* uses. . . .

I would not have done this (attend college and work on several newspaper staffs), or anything else that I did then or was to do, had it not been for my family. . . . But the most important gift my family ever gave me was the ability, and the willingness, to live as a *person* among people, and the unastonished knowledge that I could do so. Indeed, it is only at times like this, when I strip myself and stand before the mirror of self-analysis, that I become acutely conscious that the world outside myself considers me handicapped.

For though I am more visibly, more tangibly handicapped than many, I do not consider myself more handicapped than many. I with my spastically tense legs, I with the T-strap brace on my left leg, I with only the index finger of my spastic right hand helping my uninvolved left hand punch out these words on the typewriter — I am no more handicapped than you with your psychosomatic ulcer, you with your frustrated passion for power, you with your abject and quivering fear of the mushroom cloud. . . .

So, Will Shakespeare, I owe you at least a half-apology. For adversity creates the maze that leads from what we cannot do to what we can. (McKee, 1961, pp. 101-102)

Career Education Programming for Values, Attitudes, and Habits

Louis Hayward
I'm not particularly proud of what I'm doing. The shine man and I discuss it quite freely. In my own habitat I don't go around saying I'm a washroom attendant at the Palmer House. Outside of my own family, very few people know what I do. . . . No, I'm not proud of this work. I can't do anything heavy. It would be hard to do anything else, so I'm stuck. . . . Several years ago — I couldn't begin to tell you how *menial* the job was. I was frustrated with myself — for being put into that position. (Terkel, 1975, p. 155)

Barbara Terwiliger
Everyone needs to feel they have a place in the world. It would be unbearable not to. I don't like to feel superfluous. One needs to be needed. I'm saying being idle and leisured, doing nothing, is tragic and disgraceful. Everyone must have an occupation. . . . I don't mean work must be activity for activity's sake. I don't mean obsessive, empty moving around. I mean creating something new. But idleness is an evil. I don't think man can maintain his balance or sanity in idleness. Human beings must work to create some coherence. You do it only through work and through love. And you can only count on work. (Terkel, 1975, pp. 554-555)

Mike Lefevre
I got chewed out by my foreman once. He said, "Mike, you're a good worker, but you have a bad attitude." My attitude is that I don't get excited about my job. I do my work but I don't say whoopee-doo. The day I get excited about my job is the day I go to a head shrinker. How are you gonna get excited when you're tired and you want to sit down? (Terkel, 1973, p. 2)
When I come home, know what I do for the first twenty minutes? Fake it. I put on a smile. I got a kid three years old. Sometimes she says, "Daddy, where've you been?" I say, "Work." I could have told her I'd been in Disneyland. What's work to a three-year-old kid? If I feel bad, I can't take it out on the kids. . . . What does an actor do when he's got a bad movie? I got a bad movie every day. (Terkel, 1973, p. 7)

These personal reactions to important life events point up the career education mandate for helping children develop those skills needed for dealing with values, attitudes, and habits — their own and those of others. You may be thinking that these adult expressions of values and attitudes are too far removed from the thoughts and beliefs of the children you teach. Listen to these youngsters:

Billy Carpenter (Age 12)
I like my work. (Billy has been a newsboy off and on for seven years.) You know a lot of guys on your route. If you're nice, they tell everybody about how nice you are and they would pass it on. But now I'm kind of

in a hurry and I do it just any old way to get it done. 'Cause it's wintertime. It gets dark earlier. And if I don't get home in time, the stuff's cold and it ain't any good. (Terkel, 1973, p. 11)

Terry Pickens (Age 14)
    I don't see where being a newsboy and learning that people are pretty mean or that people don't have enough money to buy things with is going to make you a better person or anything. If anything, it's gonna make a worse person out of you, 'cause you're not going to like people that don't pay you. And you're not gonna like people who act like they're doing you a big favor paying you. Yeah, it sort of molds your character, but I don't think for the better. If anybody told me being a newsboy builds character, I'd know he was a liar.
    I don't see where people get all this bull about the kid who's gonna be president and being a newsboy made a president out of him. It taught him how to handle his money and this bull. You know what it did? It taught him how to hate the people on his route. And the printers. And dogs. (Terkel, 1973, p. 16)

Charlie Brown (Ageless)
Linus: What would you say you want most out of life, Charlie Brown...
    to be happy?
Charlie Brown: Oh, no . . . I don't expect that . . . I really don't — I just don't want to be unhappy. (Schulz, 1972, p. 242)

The underlying theme of these expressions is that personal values have a great deal to do with one's attitudes and behavior. Leonard Kriegel's valuing of independence and normalcy affect his attitudes toward himself and others, and they have shaped his habits or behaviors in relation to his body. Barbara Terwiliger's valuing of creative productivity is strongly reflected in her attitude towards work. Billy Carpenter values being "nice" and the security of a warm meal after work, although he finds some possible conflicts in these values. As his attitude toward his work shifts, his work habits respond to the strongest value. And then there is Charlie Brown, the lovable but pathetic little guy who values recognition, appreciation, and respect so much, but whose life experiences have shaped his attitudes to reflect low expectations for himself. All of these people have assimilated or developed their own value systems. Some of their systems work positively for them; others do not.

Career education programming for handicapped elementary school children should focus on developmental levels and the critical values, attitudes, and habits children form during the elementary years. These critical values, attitudes, and habits center upon children's self-concepts, their perception of their own value as persons, their assessment of the school experience, their valuation of effort or working, their relative desire for a "normal" life, and their hopes for the future.

The U.S. Office of Education policy paper on career education (Hoyt, 1975a) has suggested some programming assumptions for career education. Most cut across the four emphasis areas presented in the proposed school-based career education model for the handicapped (see Figure 1.3, p. 19). The following assumptions related to programming for the handicapped child in the area of values, attitudes, and habits are adapted from the Office's list of general programmatic assumptions:

1. A handicapped person's personal value system is developed to a significant degree during the elementary school years and is modifiable during those years.
2. If handicapped children can see the relationships between what they are being asked to learn and do at school and their present and future worlds outside of school, they will be motivated to learn more in school.
3. An effective means of helping handicapped children discover who they are (in a self-concept sense) and why they are (in a personal awareness sense) is helping them discover what they can accomplish in the work they do as learners, as helpers at home and school, and through productive efforts for their own benefits.
4. The basis upon which work of any kind can become a personally meaningful part of a handicapped person's life will vary greatly from one individual to another and from one stage of a life career to another. No single approach by educators can be expected to meet with universal success.
5. Positive values and attitudes toward work and good work habits can be taught effectively to most handicapped persons. Development in these areas is most effective if begun in the early childhood years.

With these assumptions in mind, I would like to suggest goals or objectives, activities, and materials to illustrate what you as a teacher or counselor can do to program for handicapped children in this area. It is outside the scope of this book to lay out a comprehensive sequential curriculum guide. Rather, I am presenting a series of representative goal or objective statements appropriate for the area of values, attitudes, and habits that provide you with specific examples of what can be done. Further, I am providing examples of activities and materials for each of the selected goal statements to give you a headstart in your own program planning in this area.

SELECTED GOAL/OBJECTIVE STATEMENTS

The following goal/objective statements are not behavioral objectives. They are, however, specific enough so that it is clear what knowledge, understanding, or performance skills are being proposed. The components dealing with conditions surrounding performance, type of evaluation, and criterion for evaluation are specific to each child's performance mode (visual/kinesthetic for auditorially impaired, auditory/haptic for visually impaired, etc.) and performance level, and should be incorporated into the basic goal statements when you develop your instructional objectives. Any of them would be appropriate for consideration in establishing objectives for a handicapped child's individualized education plan.

Goals for Values/Valuing

Primary Level (K-3)

Some important goals for handicapped children during their first three or four years in school include the following:

1. Students will demonstrate an awareness of the value of themselves as persons.

2. Students will demonstrate an acceptance of learning as a part of living.

3. Students will demonstrate acceptance of the concept of work as a part of living.

4. Students will demonstrate an understanding of leisure time or play time as a part of living for children and adults.

5. Students will demonstrate an awareness of the concept of *equal opportunity*.

6. Students will demonstrate an awareness of the concept of *responsibility*.

7. Students will demonstrate an ability to verbalize some of their own personal and social values.

Intermediate Level (4-6)

Important or critical career education goals for handicapped children in the intermediate grades build on the primary level goals. They should include the following:

1. Students will be able to demonstrate an acceptance of themselves as persons.

2. Students will be able to demonstrate an awareness of their own life career patterns to date.

3. Students will be able to identify personal traits related to success as persons and as workers.

4. Students will demonstrate an understanding of the concepts of quality of performance, equal opportunity, and responsibility.

5. Students will demonstrate an ability to verbally identify some personal and social values, prioritize them, and discuss why the value choices and rankings were made.

Goals for Attitudes

Primary Level (K-3)

The following goals for attitude development with primary-level handicapped children are important in career education programming:

1. Students will demonstrate awareness of positive and negative attitudes in characters in story books, films, sound recordings, or television programs.
2. Students will demonstrate recognition of positive attitudes at school in their own roles as learners and workers.
3. Students will demonstrate knowledge of verbal and nonverbal behaviors that reflect positive and/or negative attitudes.

Intermediate Level (4-6)

Some important goals that follow the primary level goals in the area of attitude development are:

1. Students will demonstrate ability to analyze their own attitudes toward school and their current role as workers.
2. Students will demonstrate positive attitudes toward personal success and failure.
3. Students will demonstrate an awareness of the inter-relationships among attitude, ability, experience, and performance.

Goals for Habits

Primary Level (K-3)

The following career education programming goals reflect the important role of habit development at the primary level:

1. Students will demonstrate ability to assume responsibility for themselves in meeting personal needs.
2. Students will demonstrate behavior that reflects respect for the rights of others.
3. Students will demonstrate behavior that reflects respect for the property of others.
4. Students will demonstrate behavior that reflects positive attitudes toward school and work.

Intermediate Level (4-6)

Selected goals to follow those suggested for the primary level in habit development might include the following:

1. Students will demonstrate behavior that reflects compliance with school and community standards.
2. Students will demonstrate initiative in identifying and performing tasks needing to be done.
3. Students will demonstrate cooperative behavior in school and work activities.
4. Students will demonstrate behavior that reflects the values of honesty and dependability.
5. Students will demonstrate goal-setting behaviors for themselves in school and work activities assigned.

SELECTED ACTIVITIES AND MATERIALS FOR ACHIEVING GOAL/OBJECTIVE STATEMENTS

The typical elementary teacher or counselor has many materials at his or her disposal, and activities should not be that difficult to generate. However, for purposes of illustration and stimulation of planning, I will present some selected activities and materials for most of the goal/objective statements discussed in this chapter.

Activities and Materials for Development of Values, Attitudes, and Habits

Primary Level (K-3)

Activities for the primary level (K-3) should center as much as possible on the children's immediate environment — home and school. Make-believe playing or role playing situations are helpful for acting out feelings and exploring interest areas as well as experiencing the values of other persons. Children at this level also respond to stories, recordings, films, filmstrips, television programs, songs, and manipulative play with dolls, puppets, or stuffed animals.

Nonreaders, younger children, or children with reading deficits need activities from which they can acquire information without reading for themselves. The visually handicapped child needs manipulative and auditory activities; the auditorially handicapped child needs manipulative and visual activities; and the orthopedically handicapped child needs visual and auditory activities, with manipulative experiences when possible. The learning disabled, emotionally disturbed, and mentally retarded need activities that elicit the highest degree of response, whether visual, auditory, or tactile-kinesthetic.

Materials for implementing these kinds of activities are endless. Specific examples might include:

1. *Stories and books:*

   Boxer, D. *26 Ways to be Somebody Else* (Pantheon 1960).
   Fanshawe, E. *Rachel* (Bradbury, 1975).
   Fassler, J. *Howie Helps Himself* (Whitman, 1975).
   Fujikawa, G. *Oh, What a Busy Day* (Grosset & Dunlap 1977).
   Hall, C. *I Been There* (Doubleday, 1977).
   Hart, C., Pogrebin, L. C., Rodgers, M., and Thomas, M *Free to Be . . . You and Me* (McGraw-Hill, 1974).
   Holland, J. *First Day at School* (Denison, 1968).

Jay, E. *A Book About Me* (SRA, 1969).

Johnson, S. *Value Tale Series* (Value Communications, Inc.).

Lasker, J. *He's My Brother* (Whitman, 1974).

Lenski, L. *When I Grow Up* (Lippincott, 1960).

Levine, E. *Lisa and Her Soundless World* (Behavioral Publications, 1974).

Mack, N. *Why Me?* (Children's Press, 1976).

Moncure, J. B. *All By Myself* (Children's Press, 1976).

Odor, R. *Lori's Day* (Children's Press, 1976).

Piper, W. *The Little Engine That Could* (Platt & Munk, 1976).

Project FAIS. *Hannibal Hippo Read Me A Story Series* (Educational Achievement Corporation, 1973).

———. *The Do-It Dust Factory Read Me A Story Series* (Educational Achievement Corporation, 1973).

Robinet, H. *Jay and Marigold* (Children's Press, 1976).

Rogers, F. *Mister Rogers Talks About* (Platt & Munk, 1974).

———. *Tell Me Mister Rogers About* (Platt & Munk, 1975).

Simon, N. *Why Am I Different?* (Whitman, 1976).

Stein, S. B. *About Handicaps* (Walker, 1974).

Sugarman, D. A., and Hochstein, R. A. *Seven Stories for Growth* (Pitman, 1965).

Viorst, J. *Alexander and the Terrible, Horrible, No Good, Very Bad Day* (Atheneum, 1977).

Zemach, M. *It Could Always Be Worse* (Farrar, Strauss, & Giroux, 1976).

2. *Recordings (tapes, cassettes, or discs):*

"Basic Songs for Exceptional Children" (Concept Records).

Developing Understanding of Self and Others (DUSO I) (American Guidance Service).

"Do You Know How You Grow? — Inside" (Folkways).

"Do You Know How You Grow? — Outside" (Folkways).

"Free to Be . . . You and Me" (Arista Records).

  "Getting to Know Myself" (Kimbo Educational).
  "I Like Myself" (Kimbo Educational).
  "Little Songs on Big Subjects" (Motivation Records).
  "Won't You Be My Friend?" (Lyons).

3. *Films:*
  "Beginning Responsibility: Doing Things for Ourselves in School" (Coronet).
  "Beginning Responsibility: Being a Good Sport" (Coronet).
  "Beginning Responsibility: Other People's Things" (Coronet).
  "Courtesy for Beginners" (Coronet).
  "Fairness for Beginners" (Coronet).
  "Fat Albert and the Cosby Kids" (McGraw-Hill Films).
   Note: Teaching guides accompany the above films.
  "Free to Be . . . You and Me" (Ms. Foundation).
  "Me" (Centron Films).
  "Sir Johnny On-The-Spot" (Centron Films).

4. *Filmstrips:*
  "We're Growing Up" (Eye Gate House, Inc.).
  "What Do You Think?" (School Specialty Supply, Inc.).
  "Who Do You Think You Are?" (Guidance Associates).
   Note: See section on multimedia kits for sound filmstrips.

5. *Television programs and videotapes:*
  "Fat Albert and the Cosby Kids" (Columbia Broadcasting System).
  "Mister Rogers" (Public Broadcasting Service).
  "Sesame Street" (Public Broadcasting Service).
  "Zoom" (Public Broadcasting Service).

6. *Songs:*
  Little Songs on Big Subjects (Motivation Records).
   Note: This songbook accompanies the record of the same title cited in section on records above.
  Mister Rogers' Songbook (Random House).

7. *Manipulative toys or games:*
  Commercial dolls and hand puppets.
  Homemade or crafted dolls and hand puppets.

"Helpers Three-In-One Game" (Educational Achievement Corporation).

Plush animal puppets (Childcraft).

8. *Multimedia kits:*
   Early Childhood Series (Bowmar). Books, sound filmstrips, study prints, and teacher's guide.

   First Things: Value Series (Guidance Associates). Six sound filmstrips and teacher's guide.

   "Getting to Know Me" (Society for Visual Education). Four sound filmstrips and teacher's guide.

   "Guess What Happened Today!" (Pathescope). Five color sound filmstrips with teacher's manual.

   "Guess Where We Went Today!" (Pathescope). Four color sound filmstrips with teacher's manual.

   I Am, I Can, I Will (Family Communications, Inc.). Video, audio, and print materials with suggestions for their use.

   Kindle Series; I & II (Scholastic). Sound filmstrips and teacher's guide.

   Teaching Children Values Through Unfinished Stories (Educational Activities, Inc.). Filmstrips and record album.

   The Valuing Approach to Career Education: K-2 Series (Educational Achievement Corporation). Books, sound filmstrips, games, and posters.

9. *Miscellaneous:*
   "Here I Am" (Science Research Associates). Activity books and spirit masters.

   "The Me I Know" (Science Research Associates). Activity books and spirit masters.

   Self Awareness Study Prints (Childcraft). Stimulus cards for discussion.

   Understanding My Needs Study Prints (Childcraft). Stimulus cards for discussion.

Intermediate Level (4-6)

Activities for teaching values, attitudes, and habits to handicapped children at the intermediate level can be more advanced, but must still remain at a very concrete level. These children will probably be less interested in make-believe games, but role-playing or sociodrama may appeal to them. Most children will respond to stories that they read or have read to them, as well as recordings, films, filmstrips, or games.

Language arts and social studies programs offer many unique opportunities for instruction in the values of personal responsibility, work, leisure, learning, and equal opportunity. Activities involving discussing, listening, reading, and writing about real or hypothetical situations provide a natural climate for exploring and developing values.

The sensitive teacher will also use spontaneous situations in the classroom, cafeteria, assemblies, or on the playground to identify values, attitudes, and habits that conflict with those held by others. Such value conflict situations can be used to help students become aware of their values and how those values are developed and practiced.

Keep in mind that all of the following activities for handicapped children must be geared to primary modalities for reception and expression:

1. *Stories and books:*
   Bach, R. *Jonathan Livingston Seagull* (The MacMillan Company, 1970).
   Berger, T. *I Have Feelings* (Behavioral Publications, 1971).
   Casteel, J. D. *Learning to Think and Choose* (Goodyear Publishing, 1978).
   Freeman, D. *Flash the Dash* (Children's Press, 1973).
   Hart, C., Pogrebin, L. C., Rodgers, M., Thomas, M. *Free to Be . . . You and Me* (McGraw-Hill, 1974).
   Project FAIS. *Adventures in Valuing Read-Along Books* (Education Achievement Corporation, 1974).
   ————. *The Subway Adventure Read-Along Books* (Education Achievement Corporation, 1974).

Silverstein, S. *The Giving Tree* (Harper & Row, 1964).
Williams, M. *The Velveteen Rabbit* (Doubleday & Company, 1958).
Wolf, B. *Don't Feel Sorry for Paul* (Lippincott, 1974).
2. *Recordings (tapes, cassettes, or discs):*
   Adventures in Valuing Listening Tapes (Educational Achievement Corporation).
   "Free to Be . . . You and Me" (Arista Records).
   "Little Songs on Big Subjects" (Motivation Records).
   "Secrets" (Goals, Inc.).
   The Subway Adventure Listening Tapes (Educational Achievement Corporation).
3. *Films:*
   "The Blue Dashiki: Jeffrey and His City Neighbors" (Encyclopaedia Britannica Educational Films).
   Building Work Habits Series (McGraw-Hill Films).
   "Free to Be . . . You and Me" (Ms. Foundation).
   "Good Citizens" (Encyclopaedia Britannica Educational Films).
   "He's Not the Walking Kind" (Centron Films).
   "Learning From Disappointments" (Coronet).
   "The Lemonade Stand: What's Fair" (Encyclopaedia Britannica Educational Films).
   "Leo Beuerman" (Centron Films).
   "Let's Play Fair" (Coronet).
   "They" (Centron Films).
   "You" (Centron Films).
4. *Filmstrips:*
   "The Rules We Follow" (Curtis).
   "Who Am I?" (Scholastic Kindle Filmstrips).
   Note: See section on multimedia kits for sound filmstrips.
5. *Television and videotapes:*
   "Bread and Butterflies" (Agency for Instructional Television).
   "Wonderful World of Disney" (National Broadcasting Company).
   "Zoom" (Public Broadcasting Service).

6. *Songs:*
   Little Songs on Big Subjects (Motivation Records).

7. *Games:*
   "Getting What You Want Game" (Educational Achievement Corporation).
   "School Values Auction Game" (Educational Achievement Corporation).
   "The Ungame" (The Ungame Company).
   "Work Values Auction Game" (Educational Achievement Corporation).

8. *Multimedia kits:*
   Career Survival Skills: Focus on Affective Career Education (Charles E. Merrill Company). Student worksheets, audio cassettes, in-service manual, and teacher's manual.
   Developing Understanding of Self and Others (DUSO II) (American Guidance Service). Records or cassettes, suggested activities, posters, puppet playprops, story books, discussion cards, and teacher's manual.
   Developing Basic Values Series (Society for Visual Education). Sound filmstrips.
   Focus on Self-Development, "Stage Three: Involvement" (Science Research Associates). Sound filmstrips, photoboards, pupil activities booklets, and teacher's guide.
   I Am, I Can, I Will Series, Level II (Family Communications, Inc.). Video, audio, and print materials with suggestions for their use.
   "I Am Loveable and Capable" (Argus Communications). Sound filmstrips and teacher's guide.
   "It's Your Choice" (Educational Achievement Corporation). Sound filmstrips.
   "Presenting Dynamo Power" (International Marketing Corporation). Sound filmstrips and teacher's guide.
   The Valuing Approach to Career Education: 3-5/6-8 (Educational Achievement Corporation). Books, sound filmstrips, games, and posters.

9. *Miscellaneous:*
"Being Me" (Science Research Associates). Activity books and spirit masters.
"Got to Be Me!" (Argus Communications). Stimulus cards and workbooks.

REFERENCES

Butler, A. J., and Browning, P. L. Predictive studies on rehabilitation outcome with the retarded. In P. L. Browning (ed.), *Mental retardation: Rehabilitation and counseling.* Springfield, Illinois: C. C. Thomas, 1974.

Cobb, H. V. *The forecast of fulfillment: A review of research on predictive assessment of the adult retarded for social and vocational adjustment.* New York: Teachers College Press, 1972.

Goldstein, H. Social and occupational adjustment. In H. A. Stevens and R. F. Heber (eds.), *Research in mental retardation.* Chicago: University of Chicago Press, 1964.

Henrich, E., and Kriegel, L. *Experiments in survival.* New York: Foundation for Child Development (formerly the Association for the Aid of Crippled Children), 1961.

Hoyt, K. B. *An introduction to career education.* A policy paper of the U.S. Office of Education, DHEW Publication No. (OE) 75-00504. Washington, D.C.: U.S. Government Printing Office, 1975a.

———. *Career education and the handicapped person.* Unpublished paper, Bureau of Career Education, U.S. Office of Education, Washington, D.C., 1975b.

McKee, J. D. In E. Henrich and L. Kriegel (eds.), *Experiments in survival.* New York: Foundation for Child Development (formerly the Association for the Aid of Crippled Children), 1961.

Raths, L., Merrill, H., and Sidney, S. *Values and teaching.* Columbus, Ohio: Charles E. Merrill, 1966.

Schulz, C. Charlie Brown cartoon dialogue. In J. D. Krumboltz and H. B. Krumboltz (eds.), *Changing children's behavior.* Englewood Cliffs, New Jersey: Prentice-Hall, 1972.

Stephens, B. *The development of reasoning, moral judgment and moral conduct in retardates and normals, Phase II.* Unpublished paper, Temple University, Philadelphia, 1972.

Terkel, S. *Working.* New York: Avon Books, 1975.

3

CAREER EDUCATION PROGRAMMING FOR HUMAN RELATIONSHIPS

Human relationships are the essence of social interaction. They are at the heart of the communication process linking individuals and groups. Without satisfactory human relationships, adults and children find themselves isolated or rejected by others, and they further withdraw to avoid unpleasant relations. The importance of social interaction cannot be overstated, and educators must recognize the school's role in its development.

Historically, American public schools have concentrated their efforts on educating youth in the area of academic skills. Although classroom discipline, behavior management, and meeting children's emotional needs have always been integral to the instructional process, they have been taught almost exclusively through incidental methods rather than with clearcut, purposeful objectives and procedures. Critics of public education decry this approach and advocate a humanistic philosophy that places personal and social development on an equal basis with scholastic achievement as goals for education (Illich, 1971; Phenix, 1964; Wilson, 1971).

The notion of specific, purposeful instruction in the areas of personal and social behavior has been rejected by those who see it as the responsibility of the family, religious teachers, or even as "everyone's" responsibility. Some people have the attitude that "these things come along — just let them grow up — they'll learn." Most of these people were fortunate enough to have had a childhood environment that fostered personal and social growth without specific attention to it, or they are simply insensitive to the ways children (particularly handicapped children) from different environments learn and develop values of their own.

Although the family is rightfully viewed as a prime influence on a child's personal and social development, activities with other children, particularly at school, are also important. Think back to some of your own experiences when you were in elementary school. Did you get along well with your classmates? Were you ever subjected to excruciatingly cruel treatment at the hands of your peers? Were you ever a "new kid"? Were you ever teased unmercifully because of something you were wearing or because of something you could not do? Were you ever in a fight? Handicapped children are likely to encounter most of the painful experiences we can recall for ourselves; in fact, they usually encounter even more than we did. Their "differentness" elicits overt and covert reactions from others that result in countless painful experiences. Obvious handicaps such as physical stigmata, orthopedic, visual, auditory, or speech impairments pose initial, and sometimes permanent, barriers for satisfactory social relationships. The less obvious handicaps like mild mental retardation, minor learning disabilities, or emotional disturbance, also have effects on social relationships.

According to Campbell (1964), human relationships hinge on a child's acceptance or rejection. The criteria for acceptance or rejection generally pertain to personality and social characteristics or to skills and abilities. Research evidence suggests that friendliness and sociability are associated with acceptance; social indifference, withdrawal, rebelliousness, and hostility are associated with rejection. In general, the more intelligent and creative children are more accepted by their peers; the slow learners and the retarded are less well accepted, if not outright rejected. Body size, muscular strength, maturational development, and athletic ability also seem to be criteria for acceptance.

It is easy to see that handicapped children, who typically differ from their peers in personal and social characteristics as well as in ability and skill performance, need specific instruction to deal with the special problems that will affect their acceptance or rejection. Such instruction should come from every feasible source, but in my opinion, it should come particularly from the school.

All too frequently the school's response to problems in human relationships is similar to the following excerpt from Woiwode's (1972) short story, "Don't You Wish You Were Dead":

> Bruce Stuttlemeyer was not well loved in town. He had just moved from an outlying farm into Pettibone — a village in central Illinois known for its export of peat — at the beginning of winter, and he wore bib overalls, flannel shirts, and high hook-and-eye shoes. Though his dress had been acceptable enough while he lived on a farm, he was now looked upon by his seventh grade classmates as a hick. He was diminutive and thin, with an elongated face longer than most adults', large and fleshy lips, eyebrows so blond they were invisible, and a big gap between his front teeth, one of which had the end broken off. And as if all this weren't more than enough to make him an object of derision among his classmates, who were at one of the most sensitive and snobbish of ages, he was uncircumcised and poorly endowed, and had picked up the nickname of "Needledick, the canary raper." The more he heard the name, the more wild-eyed and violent he became, and he began to attack anybody he thought was using it or mocking him in any way. Parents complained to the principal that their sons were being injured at school, and shortly after Easter vacation Bruce turned on a bully from the eighth grade who had been taunting him for days, and knocked him unconscious. He was expelled from school for a week. (p. 101)

The story describes many behaviors that should have been redirected at an earlier stage, and even when Bruce's behavior reaches its uncontrollable climax, expulsion is seen as the only solution.

In the past, elementary and secondary special education curricula have included objectives, activities, and materials focusing to some extent on human relationships. However, they have largely depended upon incidental learning to accomplish the desired ends. Rarely, if ever, has any accountability been imposed on programs, teachers, or students to monitor attainment of goals in this area. If the schools had followed a real program for such skills, perhaps there would be fewer adults with experiences like these to report:

Bruce Fletcher
I was much respected by the management, even though I drove the people that I worked with insane, because I had standards they couldn't cope with. I cannot stand laziness and neglect when I'm breaking my neck and somebody else is holding up the wall. I would scream bloody murder and carry on like a demon and a tyrant. (Terkel, 1975, p. 666)

Heather Lamb
A lot of girls (telephone operators) are painfully shy in real life. You get some girls who are outgoing in their work, but when they have to talk to someone and look them in the face, they can't think of what to say. They feel self-conscious when they know someone can see them. At the switchboard, it's a feeling of anonymousness. (Terkel, 1975, p. 66)

Harold
Things haven't gone so well with me the last few days. I am aggravated and irritated by people; my nerves are on edge. I am just blowing off excess steam, I guess. I feel like hitting some fellows. Still, I control myself as best I can. (Lindner, 1944, pp. 120-121)

Children also have stories to tell. You can probably remember having feelings like these when you were growing up:

Fourth Grade Boy
                                A Handycap Person
When I was in camp their was a girl on my bus. Her name was Jill. She could not hear or talk. On the bus she made funny sounds and looked funny but I don't think she liked it. A lot of kids made her cry because they made fun of her. One time a kid punched her in the teeth. (Bauer, 1977, p. 54).

Bradley (age 9)
If you touch me soft and gentle
If you look at me and smile at me
If you listen to me talk sometimes before you talk
I will grow, really grow.   (James and Jongeward, 1971)

What comes through in each of these quotations is a common thread of concern for understanding others, being understood, and relating in ways that positively affect one's life or career. Bruce Fletcher's anger, the social withdrawal of the telephone operators, Harold's hostility, and Bradley's plea for warm, accepting communication are typical of thousands of individuals who find so much lacking in human relationships.

Career education should include a deliberate effort to develop skills for creating and maintaining positive human relationships. Any program specifically designed for elementary-age handicapped children must deal with their special and unique problems in communicating with and understanding others. They need to learn how to communicate with non-handicapped persons and make them aware of their ignorance, naivete, or attitudes about the handicapped. They need to work through feelings of anger and hostility related to their handicaps — learning to "suffer fools gladly." They need to know how to communicate feelings about excessive assistance and denial of independence and how to deal with their tendencies to withdraw.

Planning for this approach to career education programming with handicapped children in elementary schools must have a definite structure and direction. The following premises are based in part on the general programmatic assumptions for career education presented in *An Introduction to Career Education* (Hoyt, 1975):

1. One of the most critical skill areas for the handicapped in adjustment, from childhood through adulthood, is the area of human relationships. This stems from societal attitudes toward deviance and the phenomena of stigma and stereotyping, all of which affect society's acceptance or toleration of the handicapped.
2. A handicapped person's skill in human relations is developed to a significant degree during the elementary years and is modifiable during those years.
3. Attainment of human relationships skills is a developmental process, beginning in the preschool years and

continuing into the retirement years. Maturational level and patterns may differ from age to age and from individual to individual. There may be unique differences among types of disabilities.

4. Excessive deprivation in any aspect of human growth and development can retard career development. Special variations in career development programming may be required for persons suffering significant deprivation of positive human relationships.

Career education programming in the area of human relationships is not typically cited in the literature as a discrete, identifiable component. There is a tacit assumption that it will be included, but rarely is it emphasized as a distinct area of instruction on a parallel with attitudes and values, occupational information, and acquisition of job skills. The basic assumptions presented above, particularly the last one, provide a rationale for emphasizing this area as a separate element of career education programming for the handicapped in the elementary school.

A case could probably be made for a similar emphasis in programming for the nonhandicapped, based on studies of why people leave jobs, get fired from jobs, avoid personal and social interactions in leisure time, and seek anonymity in large urban environments. If you accept this area as a legitimate component of career education programming, other educators may also move to incorporate it into their future planning.

Given these basic assumptions and this rationale for career education programming for the handicapped in the area of human relations, what specifically might be incorporated into an instructional program? Fagen and Long (1976) have proposed one curriculum approach for exceptional children in developing self-control. Self-control is defined as "one's capacity to direct and regulate personal action (behavior) flexibly and realistically in a given situation" (p. 3). From their perspective, skill in human relations can be viewed as self-control in planning and carrying out positive interpersonal behaviors and deliberate planning and effort in preventing negative interpersonal behaviors. This conscious, planned relating to others is a process based on cognitive (intellectual) and affective (emotional) responses. An instructional program should include objectives of both kinds (Crosby, 1965; Fagen and Long, 1976). The career education goals suggested below follow Fagen and Long's curriculum model, as it fits nicely into the rationale for instruction in this area.

SELECTED GOAL/OBJECTIVE STATEMENTS

These goal/objective statements are specific only insofar as they make clear what knowledge, understanding, or performance skills are being proposed. They are not stated behaviorally, because at this level of goal-setting we make no differentiation in the population we have been generally referring to as "the handicapped." The behavioral objective level would take into account specific group or individual characteristics relative to performance modality and performance level.

Cognitive Goals for Human Relations

Primary Level (K-3)

Some important goals for handicapped children during their primary grades are:

1. Students will demonstrate an awareness of behavior standards in private and public social interactions.
2. Students will demonstrate an awareness of environmental cues (signs, signals, gestures, body language, etc.) that communicate information related to others and their expectations.

3. Students will demonstrate recognition and acceptance of behavioral expectations of adults and authority figures.
4. Students will demonstrate some knowledge of similarities and differences between themselves and others.
5. Students will demonstrate an awareness of simple rules of courtesy, sharing, and cooperative play and work.
6. Students will demonstrate an awareness of behavior (positive and negative) and its consequences with peers, adults, and authority figures.

Intermediate Level (4-6)

Using the goals that should be attained at the primary level as prerequisites, goals for the intermediate level should include the following:

1. Students will demonstrate knowledge of school rules and community ordinances that relate to interpersonal relations.
2. Students will demonstrate skill in interpreting cues in the social environment that relate to behavioral expectations or interpersonal communication.
3. Students will demonstrate ability to identify and verbalize similarities and differences between themselves and others and identify critical characteristics that might facilitate or impede satisfactory relationships.
4. Students will demonstrate basic skills in self-control by developing planned actions for solving hypothetical human relations problems.
5. Students will demonstrate ability to relate actions to expected outcomes and to anticipate probable outcomes of behavior with peers, adults, and authority figures.
6. Students will show ability to follow basic rules of courtesy, sharing, and cooperation in work and play with others.
7. Students will demonstrate knowledge of the effects of prejudice and stereotyping in interpersonal relations.

Affective Goals for Human Relations

Primary Level (K-3)

In addition to the things a handicapped child should be aware of at the cognitive level, there are other important areas of development that require sensitivity and feeling. It is difficult to specify goals in this domain, but the following can serve as examples of possible goals:

1. Students will demonstrate ability to empathize with basic emotions portrayed in stories, films, sound recordings, television programs, and in real incidents at school.
2. Students will demonstrate emerging skills in self-control by managing negative feelings or emotions in interpersonal relations.
3. Students will demonstrate emerging skills in showing positive feelings toward others.
4. Students will demonstrate emerging coping skills in handling frustrating events in interpersonal relations.

Intermediate Level (4-6)

The goals and objectives for this level are primarily an extension or stabilization of the affective goals at the primary level. They should include the following:

1. Students will demonstrate emerging ability to interpret behaviors in interpersonal relations in terms of emotions, motivations, and frustrations.
2. Students will demonstrate skills in self-control by managing negative feelings or emotions in interpersonal relations.
3. Students will demonstrate skills that are age and situation appropriate in showing positive feelings toward others.

4. Students will demonstrate socially acceptable coping skills in handling frustrating events in interpersonal relations.

SELECTED ACTIVITIES AND MATERIALS FOR ACHIEVING GOAL/OBJECTIVE STATEMENTS

For an area of concern that has gained so little formal prominence in elementary school curricula, human relations probably has more available materials than any other area outside the academic subject areas. Children's literature contains so many volumes with human relations themes that special reading lists and bibliotherapies are common (Crosby, 1963; Zaccaria and Moses, 1968). In addition, human relations have been infused into reading, social studies, science, and health curricula in varying degrees from the McGuffy readers to the present. All of these sources provide a wealth of materials to draw upon.

The process of studying, working, and playing together at school provides a natural laboratory for human relations teaching, and software materials could easily play a secondary role during those "teachable moments" when a direct response is made with individuals or groups. There is an inherent trap in this approach, however, and in the past, education has succumbed to it. Using unplanned events for such instruction makes it difficult to follow any established program of specific goals and objectives. Human relations development is consequently spotty, uneven, and invariably incomplete. Materials and activities carefully selected to accomplish established goals and provide teachers with direction and structure must exist if any purposeful instruction is to occur. Spontaneous teaching can, of course, provide natural reinforcement to a planned program. The activities and materials that follow are suggested as examples for use in human relations instruction for the goals proposed earlier in this chapter.

Activities and Materials for Development of Human Relationships

Primary Level (K-3)

Since human relations development is so closely related to development of values, attitudes, and habits, both areas should receive the same basic considerations in activity and material choices for handicapped children. That is, since young children do enjoy and respond to make-believe play, listening to stories and records, watching films and television, and playing games, these activities should be used frequently. Varied activities and frequent changes in materials and media are desirable with young children, but restrictions in receptive or expressive modalities for some handicapped children will limit variation to some degree. Specific examples of some useful resources are:

1. *Stories and books:*
   Bailey, C. *Flickertail* (Walck, 1962).
   Bannon, L. *The Other Side of the World* (Houghton Mifflin, 1960).
   Berger, T. *Being Alone, Being Together* (Advanced Learning Concepts, 1974).
   Beim, J. *Swimming Hole* (Morrow, 1951).
   Bronin, A. *Gus and Buster Work Things Out* (Dell, 1975).
   Carlson, N. *Marie Louise and Christopher* (Charles Scribner's, 1974).
   Conta, M., and Reardon, M. *Feelings Between Friends* (Advanced Learning Concepts, 1974).
   ————. *Feelings Between Kids and Parents* (Advanced Learning Concepts, 1974).
   Duncan, L. *The Littlest One in the Family* (Dodd, Mead, & Company, 1960).
   Freed, A. M. *TA for Tots* (Jalmar, 1973).
   Hallinan, P. K. *That's What a Friend Is* (Children's Press, 1977).

Lasker, J. *He's My Brother* (Whitman, 1974).
Leaf, M. *Manners Can Be Fun* (Lippincott, 1958).
Martin, B. *David Was Mad* (Holt, Rinehart, & Winston, no date).
Oterdahl, J. *Tina and the Latchkey Kid* (Macmillan, 1963).
Rothschild, A. *Bad Trouble in Miss Alcorn's Class* (Scott, 1959).
Slobodkin, L. *One is Good But Two are Better* (Vanguard, 1956).
Zolotow, C. *The Hating Book* (Harper & Row, 1969).

2. *Recordings (tapes, cassettes, or discs):*
"Do You Know How You Grow? — Inside" (Folkways)
"Do You Know How You Grow?—Outside" (Folkways)
"Feelings and Emotions Through Music" (Educational Design Asociates).
First Things: Value Series (Guidance Associates).
"Free to Be . . . You and Me" (Arista Records).
"Little Songs on Big Subjects" (Motivation Records).
"Living With Others: Citizenship" (School Speciality Supply, Inc.).

3. *Films:*
"Appreciating Our Parents" (Coronet).
"Beginning Responsibility: Other People's Things" (Coronet).
"Beginning Responsibility: Rules at School" (Coronet)
"Courtesy for Beginners," 2nd Edition (Coronet).
"Fairness for Beginners" (Coronet).
"Families and Learning: Everyone's a Teacher" (McGraw-Hill Films).
"Families and Rules: Watch How Well Everything Works" (McGraw-Hill Films).
"Getting Along With Others" (Coronet).
"Me" (Centron Films).
"Our Family Works Together" (Coronet).
"People are Different, Aren't They?" (Valiant Instructional Materials Corporation). *Note:* This is a silent, color motion picture filmloop (Super 8mm).

4. *Filmstrips:*
   "About Myself," Bowmar Series, Part I (Bowmar).
   Patterns of Behavior Series (Eye Gate House, Inc.).
   "What to Do About Rules" (Guidance Associates).
5. *Television programs and videotapes:*
   I Am, I Can, I Will Series, Level I (Family Communication Inc.). "You Are Special," I-1; "Growing," I-2; "Helping," I-3; and "Feeling Happy, Feeling Mad," I-5.
   "Mister Rogers' Neighborhood" (Public Broadcasting Service).
6. *Songs:*
   Little Songs on Big Subjects (Motivation Records). *Note:* this songbook accompanies the album by the same name cited in the section on recordings.
   Mister Rogers' Songbook (Random House).
7. *Manipulative toys or games:*
   "Grow Power" (Educational Activities, Inc.).
   "The Ungame" (The Ungame Company).
   Commercial dolls and handpuppets.
   Homemade or crafted dolls and handpuppets.
   Plush animal puppets (Childcraft).
8. *Multimedia kits:*
   Becoming a Person Program (Benziger, Bruce, & Glencoe). Structured instructional program based on five themes: family, understanding yourself, maturity, relating to others, and values.
   Developing Understanding of Self and Others (DUSO I) (American Guidance Service). Records or cassettes, suggested activities, posters, puppets, puppet play props, story books, discussion cards, and teacher's manual.
   First Things Value Series (Guidance Associates). Sound filmstrips and in-service unit for teaching values.
   Focus on Self Development, "Stage One — Awareness"; "Stage Two — Responding" (Science Research Associates). Filmstrips, records or cassettes, photoboards, pupil activities books, and teacher's guide.

Human Development Program (Human Development Training Institute). Curriculum kit.

I Am, I Can, I Will Series (Family Communications, Inc.). Video, audio, and print materials with suggestions for use.

Kindle Series: III-IV (Scholastic Kindle Films). Sound filmstrips and teacher's guide.

"My Friends and Me" (American Guidance Service). Activity board, activity manual, activity pictures, magnetic shapes, story books, dolls, print blocks, audio cassettes or records, song cards, spirit masters, and teacher's guide.

Random House Program for Elementary Guidance (Random House, Inc.) Curriculum kit.

"Schools, Families, Neighborhoods" (Field Educational Publications). Filmstrips, study prints, wall charts, and teacher's guide.

Teaching Children Values Through Unfinished Stories (Educational Activities, Inc.) Sound filmstrips.

"Who Are You?" (Mafex Associates). Sound filmstrips.

9. *Miscellaneous:*

"Moods and Emotions" (Cook). Sixteen study pictures.

"Moods and Emotions of a Child's World" (Pennant Educational Materials). Eight study prints with stories, activity suggestions, and background materials.

"Social Development" (Cook). Twelve teaching pictures and twelve resource sheets.

"Understanding Our Feelings" (Leswing Press). Twenty stimulus posters and teacher's guide.

"Wally — Bertha — You" (Encyclopaedia Britannica). Puppets and activity cards.

Intermediate Level (4-6)

As handicapped children grow and mature, they usually become more sensitive about their handicaps. In normal development, the middle years of childhood (ages seven to eleven or twelve) are the years when real friendships develop among children who are classmates or neighbors. As children begin to move out from close supervision, they cannot be protected as they once were; caring parents can no longer buffer their children from others who reject or antagonize them. Handicapped children can be extremely vulnerable, and their responses to interpersonal relations depend largely on how they have learned to handle teasing, rejection, isolation, overprotection, and frustration. You cannot always assume that human relations concepts and skills have been attained simply because there are no apparent problems. Continuation of a planned instructional program in relating to others, as well as spontaneous teaching when interpersonal conflicts arise, is a necessity.

Materials and activities must be provided at the children's readiness level and must focus on their individual instructional needs within their primary learning modalities. Many, by this level, will be able to read, and the volume of such materials should be increased. Individual problems in interpersonal relations can be addressed more directly at this stage because the children will have become more independent learners. Some students, however, will continue to need your personal guidance and assistance.

Some good materials for the intermediate level are the following:

1. *Stories and books:*
   Beim, J. *Across the Bridge* (Harcourt, Brace & World, 1951).
   Bradbury, B. *Two on an Island* (Houghton Mifflin, 1965).
   Bronin, A. *Gus and Buster Work Things Out* (Dell, 1975).
   Calhoun, M. *Honestly, Katie John* (Harper & Row, 1963).
   Cleary, B. *Beezus and Ramona* (Morrow, 1955).
   Daringer, H. *Stepsister Sally* (Harcourt, Brace, & World, 1952).

DeAngeli, M. (Lofft). *Bright April* (Doubleday, 1946).
Erickson, R. *A Toad for Tuesday* (Lothrop, Lee, & Shepard, 1974).
Freed, A. M. *TA for Kids . . . (And Grown-ups Too)* (Jalmar, 1971).
Godden, R. *Miss Happiness and Miss Flower* (Viking, 1961).
Low, A. *Kallie's Corner* (Pantheon, 1966).
Muehl, L. B. *Worst Room in the School* (Holiday, 1961).
Seredy, K. *A Brand New Uncle* (Viking, 1961).
Project FAIS. *The Subway Adventure Read-Along Books* (Educational Achievement Corporation, 1974).
Yashima, T. *Crow Boy* (Viking, 1955).

2. *Recordings:*
"Danny's Song" (Family Communications, Inc.).
"Growing Up Without Sight" (Family Communications, Inc.)
"Living With Others: Citizenship" (School Speciality Supply, Inc.)
"Little Songs on Big Subjects" (Motivation Records).
The Subway Adventure Listening Tapes (Educational Achievement Corporation, 1974). *Note:* See companion books cited above.

3. *Films:*
"Developing Your Personality" (Encyclopaedia Britannica Educational Films).
"The Family — The Boy Who Lived Alone" (Encyclopaedia Britannica Educational Films).
"The Golden Rule: A Lesson for Beginners" (Coronet).
"Good Citizens" (Encyclopaedia Britannica Educational Films).
Inside/Out Series on Emotions (National Instructional Television Center).
"Let's Play Fair" (Coronet).
"Let's Share With Others" (Coronet).
"People Are Different and Alike" (Coronet).

"People Are Different, Aren't They?" (Valiant Instructional Materials Corporation). *Note:* This is a silent, color motion picture filmloop (Super 8mm).

"Problems and Attitudes in School" (Henk Newenhouse).

"Refiner's Fire" (Doubleday Multi-Media).

"Up is Down" (Goldshall).

4. *Filmstrips:*

"But It Isn't Yours" (Guidance Associates).

"Developing Your Personality" (Encyclopaedia Britannica Educational Films).

First Things Value Series (Guidance Associates). "Guess Who's in a Group?," "You Got Mad, Are You Glad?," "What Happens Between People?"

"Learning to Live Together," Part II (Society for Visual Education).

"Me, Myself and I" (Eye Gate House, Inc.).

"The Rules We Follow" (Curtis).

5. *Television programs and videotapes:*

I Am, I Can, I Will videotape cassette series, Level II (Family Communication, Inc.). "Feeling Left Out," II-6; "Having to Wait," II-8; and "Teasing and Being Teased," II-9.

Inside/Out Series on Emotions (National Instructional Television Center).

6. *Songs:*

"Little Songs on Big Subjects" (Motivation Records). *Note:* This songbook accompanies the album of the same title cited in the section on recordings above.

7. *Games:*

"Getting What You Want Game" (Educational Achievement Corporation)

"Grow Power" (Educational Activities, Inc.).

"The Ungame" (The Ungame Company).

8. *Multimedia kits:*

Becoming a Person Program (Benziger, Bruce, & Glencoe). Structured instructional program based on five themes: family, understanding yourself, maturity, relating to others, and values.

Developing Basic Values Series (Society for Visual Education). Sound filmstrips. "Respect for Property," "Consideration for Others," "Acceptance of Differences," and "Recognition of Responsibilities."

Developing Understanding of Self and Others (DUSO II) (American Guidance Service). Records or cassettes, suggested activities, posters, story books, puppets, discussion pictures, discussion guide cards, and teacher's manual.

Focus on Self Development, "Stage Three: Involvement" (Science Research Associates). Filmstrips, records or cassettes, photoboards, pupil activity booklets, and teacher's guide.

"It's Your Choice" (Educational Achievement Corporation). Sound filmstrips.

"Magic Circles" (Human Development Training Institute). Guide for human relations programming with children.

"Secrets" (Gerald Beasley). Cassettes, charts, and pamphlets.

Social Science Laboratory Units (Science Research Associates). Guide for programming.

Teaching Program with Ojemann Materials (Educational Research Council of America). Instructional resource unit.

Toward Affective Development (American Guidance Service, Inc.). Structured instructional units, discussion pictures, games, spirit masters, filmstrips, audio cassettes, posters, and teacher's manual.

Youth Dynamics (International Marketing Corporation). Filmstrips, tapes, and suggested activities.

9. *Miscellaneous:*
"Adventures of Macho and Mimi" (Human Development Training Institute). Guide for programming.
"Children and the Law" (Cook).

Resource Organizations for Materials in Human Relations

You should develop your files in such a way that new materials or services in any given area of instruction are kept up-to-date. There are a number of agencies or organizations that might provide useful information. When you ask to be placed on their mailing lists, be sure to tell them the kind of information you think would be helpful and the age/grade levels you work with. The groups listed on pages 64-67 (NSPRA, 1972) are particularly concerned with furthering human relations and may be able to provide materials and services to educators working in that area.

Several of the agencies and organizations listed have local or regional offices. There also are numerous official state, county, and municipal agencies with responsibilities in the area of human relations. (Consult your local telephone directory for addresses and telephone numbers of area resource agencies.) In addition, many state departments of education and state education associations can provide information and materials on human relations.

REFERENCES

Bauer, J. *A handycap person* (composition by a fourth grade boy). In S. Cohen, *Special People*. Englewood Cliffs, New Jersey: Prentice-Hall, 1977.

Campbell, J. D. Peer relations in childhood. In M. L. and L. W. Hoffman (eds.), *Review of child development research*. New York: Russell Sage Foundation, 1964.

Crosby, M. *An adventure in human relations*. Chicago: Follett, 1965.

————. *Reading ladders for human relations*. Washington, D.C.: American Council on Education, 1963.

Fagen, S. A., and Long, N. J. Teaching children self-control: A new responsibility for teachers. *Focus on Exceptional Children* 7(8) (1976): 1-11.

Hoyt, K. B. *An introduction to career education:* Policy paper of the U.S. Office of Education, DHEW Publication No. (OE) 75-00504. Washington, D.C.: U.S. Government Printing Office, 1975.

Illich, I. Deschooling society. In R. N. Anshen (ed.), *World perspectives*, vol. 44. New York: Harper & Row, 1971.

James, M., and Jongeward, D. *Born to win: Transactional analysis with gestalt experiments.* Reading, Massachusetts: Addison-Wesley, 1971.

Lindner, R. M. *Rebel without a cause.* New York: Grove Press, 1944.

NSPRA. *Human relations: Current trends in school policies and practices.* Washington, D.C.: National School Public Relations Association, 1972.

Phenix, P. *Realms of meaning: A philosophy of the curriculum for general education.* New York: McGraw-Hill, 1964.

Terkel, S. *Working.* New York: Avon Books, 1975.

Wilson, L. C. *The open access curriculum.* Boston: Allyn & Bacon, 1971.

Woiwode, L. Don't you wish you were dead? In E. D. Landau, S. L. Epstein, and A. P. Stone (eds.), *Child development through literature.* Englewood Cliffs, New Jersey: Prentice-Hall, 1972.

Zaccaria, J. S., and Moses, H. A. *Facilitating human development through reading: The use of bibliotherapy in teaching and counseling.* Champaign, Illinois: Stipes, 1968.

GROUPS CONCERNED
WITH FURTHERING HUMAN RELATIONS

American Civil Liberties Union
156 Fifth Ave.
New York, New York 10010

American Committee on Africa
211 E. 43d St.
New York, New York 10017

American Council on Education
One Dupont Circle
Washington, DC 20006

American Council for Nationalities
  Service
20 W. 40th St.
New York, New York 10018

American Ethical Union
2 W. 64th St.
New York, New York 10023

AFL-CIO
Department of Civil Rights
815 16th St., NW
Washington, DC 20006

American Federation of Teachers
1012 14th St. NW
Washington, DC 20005

American Friends Service
  Committee
160 N. 15th St.
Philadelphia, Pennsylvania 19102

American Indian Historical Society
1451 Masonic Ave.
San Francisco, California 94117

American Jewish Committee
165 E. 56th St.
New York, New York 10022

American Jewish Congress
15 E. 84th St.
New York, New York 10028

American Society of African Culture
101 Park Ave.
New York, New York 10017

Americans for Indian Opportunity
1820 Jefferson Pl. NW
Washington, DC 20036

Anti-Defamation League of B'nai
B'rith
315 Lexington Ave.
New York, New York 10016

Asian American Research Project
University of California
Davis, California 95616

Association on American Indian
Affairs
432 Park Ave. South
New York, New York 10016

Association of Mexican American
Educators, Inc.
26728 Rolling Vista Dr.
Lomita, California 90717

Association for Study of Negro Life
and History
1407 14th St. NW
Washington, DC 20005

Brotherhood-in-Action, Inc.
560 Seventh Ave.
New York, New York 10018

Bureau of Indian Affairs
Washington, DC 20240

Center for Urban Education
105 Madison Ave.
New York, New York 10016

Civic Education Service, Inc.
1735 K St. NW
Washington, DC 20006

Common Council for American
Unity
20 W. 40th St.
New York, New York 10018

Community Renewal Society
116 S. Michigan Ave.
Chicago, Illinois 60603

Congress of Racial Equality
200 W. 135th St.
New York, New York 10030

Council for American Unity
70 Fifth Ave.
New York, New York 10011

Council of the Southern Mountains
Berea, Kentucky 40403

Educational Heritage, Inc.
733 Yonkers Ave.
Yonkers, New York 10704

Encampment for Citizenship
2 W. 64th St.
New York, New York 10023

Folkways Scholastic Records
50 W. 44th St.
New York, New York 10036

Hispanic American Institute
100 E. 27th St.
Austin, Texas 78705

Indian Rights Association
1505 Race St.
Philadelphia, Pennsylvania 19102

International League for the
Rights of Man
777 United Nations Plaza
New York, New York 10017

Japanese American Citizens League
1634 Post St.
San Francisco, California 94115

Leadership Conference on Civil
Rights
2027 Massachusetts Ave. NW
Washington, DC 20036

65

League of United Latin American
   Citizens
P.O. Box 53587
Houston, Texas 77052

League of Women Voters of the
   United States
1730 M St. NW
Washington, DC 20036

National Association for the
   Advancement of Colored People
1790 Broadway
New York, New York 10019

National Association of Intergroups
   Relations Officials
142 Sylvan Ave.
New Haven, Connecticut 06519

National Association for Puerto
   Rican Civil Rights
939 Eighth Ave.
New York, New York 10019

National Civil Liberties Clearing
   House
1346 Connecticut Ave. NW
Washington, DC 20036

National Committee for Children
   and Youth
1145 19th St. NW
Washington, DC 20036

National Community Relations
   Advisory Council
55 W. 42d St.
New York, New York 10036

National Congress of American
   Indians
1346 Connecticut Ave. NW
Washington, DC 20036

National Congress of Parents and
   Teachers
700 N. Rush St.
Chicago, Illinois 60611

National Council of Negro Women
   Inc.
Suite 832
1346 Connecticut Ave. NW
Washington, DC 20036

National Council of Teachers
   of English
1111 Kenyon Rd.
Urbana, Illinois 61801

National Education Association
Center for Human Relations
1201 16th St. NW
Washington, DC 20036

National Indian Youth Council
3102 Central SE
Albuquerque, New Mexico 87106

National School Boards Association
Office of Human Resources
   and Minority Affairs
State National Bank Plaza
Evanston, Illinois 60201

National Urban League
55 E. 52d St.
New York, New York 10017

Philadelphia Fellowship
   Commission
Community Services Department
260 S. 15th St.
Philadelphia, Pennsylvania 19102

Public Affairs Committee
381 Park Ave. South
New York, New York 10016

Puerto Rican Research and
   Resources Center
1519 Connecticut Ave. NW
Washington, DC 20036

Science Research Associates, Inc.
Customer Service Department
259 E. Erie St.
Chicago, Illinois 60611

South Conference Educational
    Fund, Inc.
3210 W. Broadway
Louisville, Kentucky 40211

Southern Educational Foundation,
    Inc.
811 Cypress St. NE
Atlanta, Georgia 30308

Southern Regional Council, Inc.
5 Forsyth St. NW
Atlanta, Georgia 30303

Southwest Educational
    Development Laboratory
800 Brazos St.
Austin, Texas 78767

Southwestern Cooperative
    Educational Laboratory
1404 San Mateo Blvd., SE
Albuquerque, New Mexico 87108

U.S. Commission on Civil Rights
1121 Vermont Ave. NW
Washington, DC 20425

U.S. Department of Health,
    Education, and Welfare
Office of Education
400 Maryland Ave. SW
Washington, DC 20202

U.S. Department of Justice
Washington, DC 20530

Urban Coalition
2100 M St. NW
Washington, DC 20037

Women on Words and Images
P.O. Box 2163
Princeton, New Jersey 08540

4

CAREER EDUCATION PROGRAMMING FOR OCCUPATIONAL INFORMATION

Until now, career education programming has primarily emphasized occupational awareness for elementary and middle school children. In fact, for the average teacher, occupational awareness, or career awareness as it is frequently called, has become practically a synonym for career education. This is unfortunate for two reasons. First, the emphasis on occupational awareness ignores the intent of Hoyt and other career education theorists who like the word career to mean more than one's job or vocation. Second, it somehow restricts the concept of what should be taught in the area of career awareness to occupational choice alternatives. This narrow perspective not only shortchanges our children; it decelerates, if not derails, the career education movement. Certainly it negates the model of career education for the handicapped presented in this book.

Politically, there are advantages for focusing on occupational awareness in the schools. Federal and state legislators are very responsive to programs that deal with problems like unemployment and worker dissatisfaction that are so obviously visible to the public. Educationally, however, the narrow view does not make sense when we look at adult needs for occupational information that goes beyond the choice of a vocation.

This is particularly true for handicapped adults, and it is critically important that handicapped children at the elementary level be exposed to a broad perspective of occupational information during the period when they are forming lasting attitudes and perspectives on life.

Occupational information, as conceptualized here, involves knowledge of all aspects of the world of work that are critical for individuals to know about. In this chapter we will discuss some of the most critical aspects: occupational roles, occupational vocabulary, occupational alternatives, and basic information related to some realities of the world of work.

OCCUPATIONAL ROLES

Occupational Roles as a Producer

Information about producer occupational roles begins very early in a child's life through observations in the home, the neighborhood, shopping trips, and other contacts with adults. At first the roles may seem rather grossly differentiated — "Daddy works, Mommy doesn't work" — as in the case where the father is remuneratively employed and the mother is a homemaker. The next level of awareness may be that "Daddy gets paid for working, Mommy doesn't." Depending upon the adult models children have for observation, information related to roles will vary from rather simple to very complex. The simple observations lead to concrete conclusions that either everybody works, nobody works, or adults work only sometimes. The complex observations may lead children to the conclusion that some adults work all the time, some never work, some work without pay, some work seasonally, some work part time, some work at home, and many change from one type of work to another. The school's role in imparting occupational information in this area should be to present as accurately and objectively as possible the variety of occupational roles that exist. What are some of the possible occupational roles? Some of the examples just cited relate to temporal issues. That is, the roles are defined in terms of how much time a person spends in a job, or what time of day, month, or year is spent in work. Some of the information gleaned about temporal roles will be tied to family values for work. For example, some children may conclude from what they observe that working is good and therefore working all the time (steady work) must be better than working part of the time (part time, periodic, or seasonal work). This value can be picked up easily from parents or adult models who believe that a full-time worker role is better than a part-time worker role. Obviously, this is a rather simple espousal of the Protestant work ethic and if occupational roles are evaluated in light of the needs and purposes of the workers themselves and the supply and demand for labor, the implications become far more complex. The presentation of some occupational information is closely tied to the issue of values (discussed in Chapter 2), which makes it difficult to teach career education concepts in discrete, mutually exclusive categories.

What other kinds of roles exist? One way of categorizing roles might be to place them in general categories related to the focus of the work, like those who work with people, with things, or with ideas. Another approach would be to divide jobs on the basis of paid versus unpaid work. Or, roles could be sorted according to location — indoor workers, outdoor workers, city workers, country or rural workers, etc. Worker roles can also be viewed in terms of producers, consumers, maintainers, disposers, and recyclers. Still another way to look at roles would be to put them in service categories — health workers, transportation workers, construction workers, agriculture workers, manufacturing workers, entertainment workers, government workers, etc. This approach has been used for the U.S. Office of Education Occupational Clusters (Clark, 1974; Weagraff, 1973). See Appendix B for examples of occupations in each USOE cluster.

71

However producer roles are viewed, the important thing to remember is that handicapped children need an information base for their own roles in their career development and should be encouraged to try out roles in play activities, classroom activities, and work-related assignments. A deliberate effort should be made to keep children free from stereotyped roles related to their disability, sex, or racial identity.

Occupational Roles as a Consumer

Everyone plays the role of consumer in the world of work at some time; handicapped children, depending upon the severity of their handicap, probably experience more as a consumer than a producer early in their lives. In fact, handicapped children and their parents may believe that the consumer role is the only one available. Each of us must make an individual value judgment about what, if any, producer role we will play, but the consumer role is virtually inescapable in our society. For the handicapped, there may be less choice than for the nonhandicapped, and the consumer role frequently is the only role they are permitted to experience.

It is the responsibility of the school to provide occupational information for both roles. The whole career education movement has been conceptualized primarily as a means of educating our children for the producer or worker role. Again, the obvious assumption of this approach is that being a worker/ producer is good for the individual and for society. What is not verbalized is the message that being a consumer only is *not* good for the individual or society. Educators of the handicapped have a special responsibility to design curricula that will provide opportunities for learning and career development not restricted to the role of producer as *paid* worker.

Farber (1968) has theorized that the American work structure is based on a system of "slots" that must be filled to keep it functioning. The number of slots varies according to the national economy and supply-demand factors for each of the types of slots available. The people who fill those slots are selected on the basis of varied employer criteria. Farber describes those who are not selected as a "surplus population," comprised basically of the poor, the untrained, the physically and mentally handicapped, the elderly, and convicted felons and other "deviant" or "incompetent" persons. Although some individuals manage to move in and out of the surplus population, the majority remain there or, at best, spend only a minor proportion of their time filling a slot.

Farber's theory is somewhat pessimistic for the handicapped, and it forces us to consider the question, "If the handicapped are going to be largely excluded from the work force, what will their roles be in our society?" Obviously, they must all continue to be consumers and may spend a majority of their time in that role. As Hoyt (1975b) has stated:

> The cosmopolitan nature of today's society demands that career education embrace a multiplicity of work values, rather than a single work ethic, as a means of helping each individual answer the question, "Why should I work?" (p. 4)

An occupational information program, then, should provide learning experiences that will result in new or expanded awareness of possible career roles. In the area of producer/worker roles, there should be an emphasis on the possibility of being productive though unpaid, as with the "work" of the student as a learner, the work of the volunteer, and work activities that are part of daily living or leisure time. In the area of consumer roles, appreciation should be cultivated for those whose work and productivity have made possible the services, conveniences, or environments that are available. Further, elementary children need to begin learning how to use such services efficiently and effectively.

OCCUPATIONAL VOCABULARY

Students need to develop or expand their vocabularies if they are to acquire basic information about their present and future occupational roles. This is somewhat parallel to first-year law or medical students, who spend the first few months of training learning the "language" of their profession. They must acquire up to 20,000 new words during their special schooling. The task facing most elementary handicapped children is not so monumental, but they do have to establish hearing vocabulary skills,* which are essential for acquiring any meaningful occupational information. When possible, reading vocabulary skills for acquiring the necessary concepts or facts are also desirable.

Vocabulary development is necessary for understanding concepts about work roles, learning what occupations exist, and discovering something about the characteristics of work and work settings. For example, if you wanted to teach primary children a lesson or unit on the concept of authority hierarchies, essential vocabulary might include the following terms:

boss	worker	employee
owner	employer	aide
helper	in charge	

If you wanted to teach a lesson on the same concept to sixth graders, essential vocabulary might include these additional terms:

director	chief	executive
coordinator	tradesman	administrator
superintendent	partner	supervisor
operator	subordinate	service personnel
gang	foreman	self-employed
hand	crew	deputy
assistant	head	work people
staff	laborer	right-hand man

---

*For hearing impaired children, the term "hearing vocabulary" is meant to include information received via lip-reading, manual communication, or total communication.

Within the consumer role, if you wanted to teach vocabulary related to the concept of being one for whom a service is provided, the following words might be appropriate for the first or second grade level:

customer   patient   audience
buyer

Fifth or sixth graders might need to know these additional words:

purchaser   renter   voter
consumer   user   patron
passenger   client   member
buyer   shopper   citizen

Increasing vocabulary to enhance awareness of occupational alternatives helps children move from early childhood descriptors of occupations or workers — "store man," "telephone man," and "office lady" — to the correct terminology — "sales clerk," "telephone installer," . . . "secretary," or "office manager." In addition to teaching children the correct terms for occupations they already know about, they should also be exposed to new words for new or unfamiliar occupations. Comprehension of the vocabulary words should be based on a knowledge of the essential functions of the various occupations.

Perhaps the most difficult vocabulary to teach is that which relates to the abstract concepts of the characteristics or realities of work and work settings. Again, there can be a continuum of difficulty corresponding to the stages of introduction. If you want to stay at the concrete level, using verbal descriptors with primary children to discuss the occupation of a nurse, you might introduce or review the meanings of words like these:

temperature   injection   chart
medication   prescription   walker
sterilize   blood pressure

At the intermediate level, more technical and abstract vocabulary concepts might be needed to describe a nurse's work or work setting:

technical	malpractice	administrative duties
records	medical ethics	aide supervision

The important thing to keep in mind is that attitudes, values, and knowledge are based on language. If we expect students to understand what we want them to learn, they must be able to know and use the words that are basic to our objectives. Obviously, many handicapped children have language deficits. Teaching occupational information to children with language deficits poses a problem, but it is not at all an impossible task.

OCCUPATIONAL ALTERNATIVES

When does the process of considering occupational alternatives begin? Certainly it begins before children ever begin their formal education. From the time children first hear the ditty, "rich man, poor man, beggar man, thief; doctor, lawyer, merchant, chief," they are exposed to the concept of occupational and lifestyle alternatives. If they do not hear this popular verse, they are exposed in a variety of ways to the same concept. Nursery rhymes ("Rub-A-Dub-Dub," "Pat A Cake," "The Lamplighter," and others), children's books and stories, toys, and television all provide early, though sometimes distorted or biased, perceptions of occupational alternatives.

Educators of handicapped elementary school children should have some perspective on occupational choice theory as it relates to normal growth and development before they get too deeply involved in any one type of special programming for their children. There are, of course, a number of theories, but we will look at just one in brief as a general base. Ginzberg and his associates (Ginzberg, Ginsburg, Axelrad, and Herma,

1951) have studied the occupational choice process and concluded that it is a developmental process. They believe it is a series of decisions made over a period of years, with each step meaningfully related to what has been decided before. They hold that the entire process ends in a compromise among many factors. Some people have to compromise little, others a great deal.

The Ginzberg theory suggests that the occupational decision-making process occurs in three basic stages — fantasy, tentative choice, and realistic choice. The particular stage of interest for us is the fantasy stage. Ginzberg and his associates conceptualize it as the first ten to twelve years of an individual's life. They contend that children begin to think during this period in terms of their desire to be adults; they believe that they can be anything they want to be. Their choices of adult occupational roles are arbitrary, changeable, and ordinarily made without reference to reality. The nature of these choices is limited by their environments and by their capacities for productive thinking. Even though children may not verbalize their fantasies during this period, their play activities give important clues as to what roles or what values about work or work-related factors (wealth, power, fame, independence, etc.) they are considering. Teachers and parents should not be alarmed when children play games involving occupational roles that are socially unacceptable (gambler, robber, gangster, etc.), unless the fascination persists into adolescence or the skills and functions of the role are obviously the child's primary aspiration.

Typically, when children fantasize, they are playing out the desire to live a life that appears exciting, glamorous, or powerful. This is usually done without any regard to personal, social, or legal consequences. In a way, they are using play to express the kinds of persons they see themselves as being, but they also are doing it without much conscious awareness of what it means. By way of personal example, my first remembered occupational fantasy (at age six or seven) was that of missionary. This choice was a consequence of listening with rapt attention to a talk given by a missionary. Obviously, I had no way of knowing what a missionary actually did, but certain meanings associated with the occupation had appeal — doing "good" things, being admired, and traveling in faraway lands. My last childhood fantasy (at age thirteen) was to be president of the United States (no less). In that instance, I was influenced by the 1948 presidential election. Again, the choice was based on the most meager information about what the president actually did. My perceptions that the president obviously did "good" things, traveled, and was liked by, if not everybody, at least a majority of the people, was strong, and served as reasonable justifications for the serious declarations made to friends and family.

In both of the examples described above, some continuing occupational values emerge. That is, from age six or seven to age thirteen, the occupational choice changed, but the perceived attributes of the two occupations did not change — i.e., a desire for doing something worthwhile, traveling, and wanting some degree of prestige or feeling of being admired. Those who know me will recognize the persistence of these values to this day and their significance in my current occupation, although opportunity to travel has been the only value realized with certainty.

How long should occupational fantasies last? Later in life, fantasies still occur, but usually with much more awareness of one's abilities, interests, goals, and the social implications of the alternatives in satisfying those fantasies. For example, one man in the advertising business has stated in an interview appearing in *Working* (Terkel, 1975):

> I have an active fantasy life — not during the workday, because it's coming at me so fast. Many of my fantasies have to do with the control of society. Very elaborate technological-type fantasies: a benign totalitarianism controlled by me.
>
> Actually, my career choice in advertising, which I've drifted into, is connected with the fantasy of power. (p. 118)

Perhaps most of us have a Walter Mitty fantasy life, especially if reality has not been matched with the dreams and fantasies of the past or present. The point to be made is that children naturally develop their fantasies and some of them relate very specifically to occupations. All children who have the intellectual ability to think or talk about what they want to be someday believe they can be whatever they want to be. They somehow make an arbitrary translation of their needs into an occupational choice without much awareness of why the choice is made in relation to their interests, abilities, or values. They are usually stimulated by events, activities, or experiences that present some strong role model in that occupation. They generally persist in a choice until a new, more appealing one comes along or until verbal or nonverbal "put-downs" from peers or adult authority figures dampen their enthusiasm.

In spite of the normal tendency for young children to fantasize freely, there is some evidence to suggest that these fantasies or early aspirations are influenced by sex and ethnic background. For example, sex differences in personal characteristics of white children appear very early in their games and activities. Girls' games usually involve low risk, taking turns, indirect competition, accommodation, and inclusiveness. Boys' games emphasize high physical risk, physical contact, intrusiveness, and competition leading to a clear designation of winners and losers (Lee and Gropper, 1974; Sutton-Smith, 1972). From toddler days, boys are expected to develop physical, "doing" competencies, while girls are encouraged to develop interpersonal sensibilities and skills (Baumrind, 1972; Maccoby and Jacklin, 1974).

Even without specific information about occupations, girls in the early grades seem to get the idea that they are limited. There is little in the research literature concerning this phenomena for preschool girls, but there is evidence that in the primary grades girls show a far narrower range of aspired-to occupations than do boys. Most studies report that boys select two to three times as many different occupations as girls and that roughly two-thirds of the girls at this age level choose either teacher or nurse (Boynton, 1936; Clark, 1967; Deutsch, 1960; Looft, 1971; Nelson, 1968; Siegel, 1973). From kindergarten through the sixth grade, girls report that women can work only in certain occupations — like nurse, secretary, waitress, or librarian — but men are not similarly restricted

(Schlossberg and Goodman, 1972), and it is much more common for girls to suggest that spouse and parent will be their major occupational roles as adults.

The effects of ethnic or minority group status are generally less clear and not obviously differentiated among the major minority groups within the United States. In fact, when social class and intelligence are held constant, aspirations may be higher for blacks than for whites (Barnett and Baruch, 1973; Boyd, 1952; Nelson, 1968). There is also some evidence to indicate that black children, and presumably other minority group children, may devalue their own group in comparison to whites (Crooks, 1971) and that black children underestimate their own abilities to advance educationally and to enter high status professional occupations (Wylie, 1963). Thus, for minority children, we do not see the same early acceptance of lower occupational attainment that we saw for girls, although there may be a similar pessimism about their own competencies. Undoubtedly, both groups (girls and minority group children) come to an early recognition of the stereotyped and discriminatory patterns of occupational attainment among adults they know, and this must somehow affect their own aspirations, expectations, and fantasies (Leifer and Lesser, 1976).

Another consideration in occupational alternatives is the effect of the "put-down," or negative response from a peer, sibling, parent, or any adult authority figure. This is one of the most devastating experiences a child can have. It is much more of an obstacle to performance than actual failure experiences. Since elementary teachers, counselors, and administrators must be highly sensitive to this as they begin to deal more and more directly with mentally and physically handicapped children and their parents, some emphasis is given here to the whys and hows of put-downs.

Why would anyone deliberately put down a handicapped child? In most instances of such interactions among children, the put-downs are the result of jealousy for special treatment or attention, an attempt to clearly establish the handicapped child's position in the group as a dependent (a low-status, "be thankful you are included" attitude), or an ignorant (but well-meant) catering to the abilities and feelings of the handicapped child. With adults, put-downs are probably more often attempts to protect, provide for, and "educate" the child to the realities of the world. In any case, whether or not a remark or nonverbal communication is intended to be helpful, it is frequently interpreted as a put-down by the handicapped child.

Handicapped children moving through the fantasy stage of occupational choice can meet with put-downs in a number of ways. Consider the following examples:

A learning disabled child says, "I want to be a teacher." Another child in the class giggles and says, "You can't even read. How do you expect to be a teacher?"

A visually handicapped child says, "When I grow up I want to be a disc jockey." A teacher says, "I don't think you could do that without being able to see. How about something you can make with your hands without being able to see?"

A mildly retarded child says, "I'm going to be a pro football player." A physical education teacher says, "You've got to know hundreds of plays and patterns in pro football. I don't think you could do that."

An orthopedically handicapped child says, "I want to be a steel worker like my Dad." A classmate says, "You've got to be strong and tough to do that. I could do that, not you."

A deaf child signs to his parents, "I want to work at a funeral home." His mother shudders and grimaces.

Frequently, such put-downs of handicapped children result from a lack of information or from distorted information about either the potential of a child or of the demands and requirements of the occupation for which a child has indicated a preference. Stereotyping of the handicapped as persons and stereotyping of job characteristics can both operate in the put-down of a child's declarations. When one considers as well the unpredictability of performance from childhood to adulthood and some of the traditional stereotyping of persons and jobs on the basis of sex, it is easy to see how our social values and attitudes can impinge on the self-concepts of handicapped children.

All children, but especially mentally and physically handicapped children, need to be able to fantasize about their future roles or occupational identities like normal children. Most professionals in the field of occupational development start with the assumption that occupational choices begin and end (over a period of years) with people trying to satisfy the most important of their personal needs (Crowne and Stephens, 1961; Englander, 1960; Super, 1963; Wylie, 1961). In doing this, a number of compromises have to be made. The young handicapped child at the elementary school level rarely, if ever, states an occupational goal to meet any personal need other than that of self-esteem. Referring again to the hierarchy of needs suggested by Maslow (1954) — survival, safety or security, belonging or love, esteem, and self-actualization — the first three basic needs are usually being met by someone else's efforts. Statements about wanting to be a policeman, astronaut, pilot, teacher, or nurse relate to the children's needs to be esteemed for *who they are* or, at least, *who they are going to be.* When they assume occupational roles in play, they see themselves as *being* adults in various roles right now. When they make statements of intent, they are compromising with the reality of age, but they are still seeking the positive feeling of esteemed for *who they are* or, at least, *who they are going to be.* (1951, p. 194) has stated: "In expressing a vocational preference, a person puts into occupational terminology his idea of the kind of person he is."

Career education must be particularly responsive to handicapped children's needs for self-esteem. There is plenty of time later for facing the realities they must accept in regard to who and what they will be. The idea is to make children as aware as possible of occupational alternatives, while continually accepting their declarations (regardless of how bizarre or inappropriate they may seem), thus affirming them as persons.

BASIC INFORMATION RELATED
TO SOME REALITIES OF THE WORLD OF WORK

The difficulty in providing occupational information to elementary aged children is that you will be trying to encourage your pupils to want to work and to be a worker, but you will also have to be honest in pointing out some of the realities of work that may be negative. Attitudes, values, and habits that are important in career development are difficult to teach without getting into some of the areas that may foster negative or unacceptable attitudes and behaviors. This section deals with some of the realities that are especially important for handicapped children to learn about. Positive or negative, they are the prevailing rules of the game that have been established by the people of influence and power in our society.

Reality #1

In North America in general, and in the United States in particular, society is work-oriented. It values work and those who are workers. Although no one can be directly compelled to work in our society (except those who are ordered by the courts to labor as a punishment for some crime), there are many formal and informal pressures operating to "make" people into workers. From a very early age, children are bombarded with messages designed to convince them that work is not only necessary to obtain "good things" — material goods, independence, respect, mobility, etc. — but also something good in itself. Parents, teachers, and even the church are conveyors of the message:

Parents: "If you will work for me this afternoon you can earn $1.00 to buy that toy you want."

Teachers: "If you learn how to read, you can get a job some day and be somebody."

Church: An old Protestant hymn has a verse that goes:

> I sing a song of the saints of God
> Patient and brave and true,
> Who toiled and fought and lived and died,
> For the Lord they loved and knew.
> And one was a doctor, and one was a queen,
> And one was a shepherdess on the green;
> They were all of them saints of God, and I mean,
> God helping, to be one too!

In addition to institutionalized forces like the family, the schools, the media, and the church, our social folklore points to the rewards and virtue of work. Fictional accounts of "poor boy making good," Benjamin Franklin's maxims, biographical accounts of famous people who made good by working hard, and even folksongs influence children to become willing workers. If, in spite of all these formal and informal forces, the child grows to physical maturity with little or no motivation to work or is even hostile toward work, he or she is soon made aware of a host of social punishments and deprivations. For most of us, the system is so effective that unemployment produces high levels of personal guilt, anxiety, and feelings of worthlessness. For the handicapped, these feelings are heightened, even though they may be able to intellectualize that factors beyond their control are responsible.

Neff (1968) has discussed some trends in changes in the meaning of work that are important because the trends are even stronger now, ten years after he made the following statement:

> Many observers of the contemporary social scene (e.g., Bell, 1956; Riesman, 1950; Whyte, 1956; Goodman, 1960) appear to be convinced that the work-oriented cultural pressures we have been discussing were far more characteristic of the nineteenth century than of the twentieth and that new pressures antagonistic to the work-culture are arising. These writers express alarm that a rapidly advancing technology is rendering many kinds of work so routinized and mechanical that there is an acute danger that work is becoming meaningless to those who perform it. Further it is pointed out by some (Harrington, 1962) that

increasingly stable "pockets of poverty" are producing a situation in which successive generations of people are excluded from the work-culture and in which children grow to maturity without any of the normal cultural pressures and inducements to acquire the motivation to work. Many other components of contemporary society also serve to balance the overwhelming force of the compulsion to work: the long-run secular trends toward shortening of the working day and working week, the increasing emphasis on recreation and self-development, the moderating influence of the trade unions and the gradually widening conception that labor is a salable commodity like any other and thus neither a mission or a duty. On balance, however, the work-orienting forces in our culture appear still to be far stronger than those which press against it, although the latter have the potential of becoming major problems for the industrial society of the future. (p. 127)

Even though the past ten years have shown more indications of work alienation, a rising "leisure ethic," and increasing numbers on welfare funds, the traditional meaning of work is still held by the power structure and still espoused by our major societal institutions. As long as this is true, the reality should be communicated to children.

Reality #2

Work, whether paid or unpaid, occurs in a particular locale: the factory, the store, the office, the construction site, the shop, the clinic, the home. Work can occur in the home — artist, writer, telephone answering service, etc. — but by and large a person must go out to work. This reality has two important implications for the handicapped. First, one must be mobile in order to get to work. This requires a set of competencies for travel. Choices of work may be strongly influenced by this reality alone. The second implication is that if work most frequently occurs away from home, it takes place in a public setting. A public place limits privacy and usually has a set of expected behaviors; there are often formal or informal standards for dress and social amenities.

Children need to learn that a work setting is not a place of play or relaxing. Children with mental or physical handicaps need to learn skills for traveling to work and need to know that once they get there, they will be expected to act in certain appropriate ways for that particular setting. They should begin to learn at the elementary level that these expectations for behavior will vary from one setting to another. This may be confusing to some, but it should be an appealing content area for a lesson or unit on any occupation or occupational cluster.

Reality #3

Paid work is largely impersonal. Unpaid work may or may not be impersonal, depending upon the nature of the work. Thus, the personalized relationship associated with play, recreation, or a loving relationship is not expected on a job. In fact, it may be forbidden. This is one reality that children may have already been exposed to indirectly at home, as when they detect different expectations from a parent depending on whether the tone of voice *asks* or *tells* the child to perform a household chore. The child experiences the parent as a "boss" with certain expectations about *what* is to be accomplished, *how* it is to be accomplished, and *how well* it was accomplished. The parent temporarily becomes an impersonal work supervisor and acts out a role that is basically the norm in the work world.

The reality of impersonality and working with and for relative strangers who are "all business" may be discouraging to children who have strong needs for more personal relationships. Exposing them to this reality runs the risk of their being turned off to the notion of working, but you will do them even more of an injustice if you ignore the reality, or worse, distort it so that they build up unrealistic expectations.

Reality #4

Work has its reward systems. Paid work obviously has the reward of remuneration, but unpaid work may provide the reward of saving money — that is, not having to pay someone else to do the work. There are other rewards of work, however, that should be mentioned. Some people see work as having the benefit of being of service, an opportunity to pursue interests and abilities, a means of meeting and interacting with people, a way of avoiding boredom, or a chance to gain or maintain self-respect or esteem.

Children need to know that people work for other things besides money. The question, "What's in it for me?" is not inappropriate for children who are learning to sort out values and acquiring a base for verbalizing, "I want to work because..."

Reality #5

Work is bound by time. Most workers have starting times and ending times. Certain times are set aside for breaks, for eating, or for clean-up. Many jobs are based on payment for certain hours with extra payment for overtime. Even when pay is based on "piece rate," the individual is racing against time to produce or complete as many pieces as possible. There are job benefits that relate to time off and there are penalties or sanctions against being late. To waste time at work is always frowned upon and if it is a chronic behavior, it may be grounds for removal from the job.

It is clear that an inability to exercise self-discipline in the area of time is one of the most serious obstacles to adjustment to work. This is often difficult for children to understand, especially when they learn that parents and teachers are indulgent and tolerant with respect to the way children spend their "free" time. Thus, although you may rebel with the children somewhat and appreciate their resistance to this domination of their behavior, the reality is there and they must learn to understand the system and possible alternatives to it.

Reality #6

Work is seldom performed in complete isolation or independence. Most work involves two or more people who interact

in various ways. One of the most important of these interactions is that of worker and supervisor. Other important interactions are those of worker and worker, and worker and consumer (customer, patient, client, etc.). Still another is the interaction of the worker and subordinates. Depending upon the size
and complexity of the work setting, the interpersonal reactions
required may be more critical to staying on that job than the
ability to perform the work tasks.

There may not be a formal communication of expected
behaviors in work interactions, but they are communicated,
nevertheless, perhaps through modeling, worker "grapevines,"
or events that illustrate the rewards or penalties workers can
expect in the system.

There is a definite parallel between this area of work world
reality and what children experience in school. There is no
question that pupils quickly develop some informal standards
of behavior for themselves. While this is occurring, the teacher
is trying to establish both formal and informal "rules" to define pupil-teacher interactions. The child who is seen as different, obnoxious, or as a convenient target for teasing, can be
made miserable by peers in a hundred ways. Children should
be prepared for a continuation of this reality in their future
work settings. They need to learn the basic expectations so they
can develop a balanced response system of dependence and
independence in job performance (worker-supervisor interactions) and in intimate and casual job relations (employee-
fellow worker and employee-consumer interactions).

Reality #7

Work settings rarely exist in isolation. As societies have
become more industrial, there has been an increasing dependence and interdependence among workers and work groups.
Producers of goods require the services of workers in raw
materials, manufactured goods for tools and equipment, transportation workers, marketing and distribution workers, and
business and office personnel on a continuous basis. Periodi-
cally they may require the services of workers in the building

trades, communication and media, health, and public service. Likewise, any one of these work groups will have dependent or interdependent relationships with one or more of the others.

Children at the elementary school level can and should become aware of these relationships to understand the importance of all types of work groups and to combat some of the occupational stereotyping and status problems that inevitably arise in a study of the world of work and their own fantasies about being a part of it.

Reality #8

Not everyone who wants to work can obtain work nor can everyone who obtains work be employed in a work of their choice. This reality is one that may affect all workers, but especially the mentally and physically handicapped. At the elementary level, however, this reality should be presented as a general issue rather than a particular one for them. As stated earlier, they should be allowed to have their fantasies about being various kinds of workers; too much reality at this stage would be inappropriate. Withholding some reality orientation from them on this topic is advisable, because although the facts show that the handicapped as a group may be adversely affected, they are not accurate predictors for any one handicapped individual.

The reality of not everyone being able to work may already be "overlearned" by some pupils. The current unemployment rate is clear evidence of this reality and many school children have experienced it in their families. It is also likely that a majority of pupils have witnessed parents or family members who are not satisfied with their work and would be in another work setting if they felt they had a choice. In *Working*, Terkel (1975) described his perception of the issue in these words:

> This book, being about work, is, by its very nature, about violence — to the spirit as well as to the body. It is about ulcers as well as accidents, about shouting matches as well as fist-fights, about nervous breakdowns as well as kicking the dog around. It is above all (or beneath

all), about daily humiliations. To survive the day is triumph enough for the walking wounded among the great many among us.

For the many, there is a hardly concealed discontent. The blue-collar blues is no more bitterly sung than the white-collar moan. "I'm a machine," says the spot welder. "I'm caged," says the bank teller, and echoes the hotel clerk. "I'm a mule," says the steelworker. "A monkey can do what I do," says the receptionist. "I'm less than a farm implement," says the migrant worker. "I'm an object," says the high-fashion model. Blue collar and white call upon the identical phrase: "I'm a robot." (pp. xiii, xiv)

Part of the dissatisfaction with work comes from problems with status or prestige. The prestige hierarchy of occupations is one of the most studied aspects of the stratification systems of modern societies. Interestingly, the consensus of the investigators is that prestige hierarchies are similar from country to country and from subgroup to subgroup. Further, there is stability in the prestige hierarchies over time. Hodge, Siegel, and Rossi (1966) found the following occupations most often included in the top ten and bottom ten occupations:

Top Ten	Bottom Ten
U.S. Supreme Court Justice	Taxi Driver
Physician	Farm Hand
Nuclear physicist	Janitor
Scientist	Bartender
Government scientist	Clothes-presser in a laundry
State governor	Soda fountain clerk
Cabinet member in the federal government	Sharecropper
College professor	Garbage collector
U.S. Representative in Congress	Street sweeper
Chemist	Shoe shiner

This is not a current, definitive list by any means. It contains some occupations that are nearing obsolescence (soda fountain clerk, street sweeper, and shoe shiner) and it reflects the forced choices included in the National Opinion Research Center's list of ninety occupations used for the study. What it does indicate is that people do have definite opinions about the prestige factors of occupations and are in high agreement on any list.

Children become sensitized early to adult evaluations of occupations and learn to use such information when appropriate in their play or in conversations with peers and adults. It appears to be so characteristic of human behavior to classify, rank, and establish "pecking orders" that it is futile for schools to attempt to do battle with the prestige hierarchy system. Nonetheless, if work dissatisfaction is related to occupational prestige, educators need to be alert to possible bias in curriculum materials, in responses to students' questions or statements about occupations, and certainly in selection of resource persons to come to the class and talk about their work.

Another factor in worker dissatisfaction is the general feeling of lack of control over one's life, particularly as it relates to occupational choice. Miller and Form (1951, p. 185) address this issue in their statement that "accident is the deciding factor in the determination of the occupation of most workers." The "accident" they refer to is the accident of birth. The social factors that affect vocational development, according to most researchers and theorists, include social class, economic status, race, parental motivations for children's education, sibling rivalry, schooling, type of community, and pressure groups like military service recruiters (Lipsett, 1962).

Thus, although it is true that many people take no active part in their occupational choices and let circumstances dictate their futures, there are countless individuals who have overcome the forces of social class, home background, physical and mental handicaps, race, or sex to achieve personal satisfaction. How they accomplish this is not completely documented, but from the available evidence (Henrich and Kriegel, 1961) they apparently managed to attain the awareness of the "real" world and the attitudes and skills needed to solve problems, seek alternatives, and achieve their goals.

The elementary school has got to provide a stimulating, nurturing environment for all children to learn and grow in understanding the demands and expectations of the work world.

By now it should be obvious that many of the critical components of the work personality are formed during the elementary school years. Many of the demands of the worker role are first encountered in the school setting. The child gets his or her first serious conditioning to the clock and structured time; there is a continuing pressure to achieve and produce; he or she must learn to adapt to all kinds of strangers (teachers, visitors, and classmates); and he or she must begin the process of adapting to the public and impersonal aspects of life. The handicapped child in particular needs to be specifically directed to occupational information related to occupational roles, occupational vocabulary, occupational alternatives. Basic information related to the realities of the world of work must be taught purposefully. Depending on incidental learning in these areas is tantamount to malpractice.

Your planning for purposeful, systematic career education programming in the area of occupational information for the mentally or physically handicapped children in your school should be based on a philosophy similar to that behind programming for nonhandicapped children. As in previous chapters, I now offer a set of basic premises based, in part, on the general programmatic assumptions for career education presented in *An Introduction to Career Education* (Hoyt, 1975a):

1. Occupational roles, occupational vocabulary, awareness of occupational alternatives, and basic information on some of the realities of work can be taught to and learned by mentally and physically handicapped children. Handicapped children can effectively use such skills, once learned, to enhance their career development.

2. Occupational roles for the handicapped will vary over a lifetime. They need specific information on both producer and consumer roles.

3. Specific occupational choices represent only one category of choices involved in career development. The choices made by handicapped children do get more realistic as they move from childhood to adulthood,

but the rate of change may be slower than for the nonhandicapped. To some degree, choices are modifiable during most of one's adult years.

4. Occupational decision-making is accomplished through the dynamic interaction of limiting and enhancing factors, both within the individuals and in their present and proposed environments. It is not, in any sense, a simple matching of individuals with jobs, especially the handicapped.

5. Occupational stereotyping hinders full freedom of occupational choice for the handicapped and other minority groups. These restrictions can be reduced to some extent through programmatic intervention strategies begun in the early years.

6. The same general strategies used in reducing worker alienation in industry can be used to reduce worker alienation among pupils and teachers in the classroom.

Using these assumptions as a base for thinking and planning for handicapped children in the area of occupational information, consider the series of representative goal/objective statements that follow. They should serve as examples from which you can brainstorm dozens more for individuals or groups for whom you have programming responsibility. Following the goal/objective statements, examples of activities and materials for accomplishing these and related objectives are also presented.

SELECTED GOAL/OBJECTIVE STATEMENTS

The following goal/objective statements, like those in previous chapters, require more specification to make them behavioral. They should provide you with a feel for the setting of objectives in the area of occupational information. Separate goal statements will be presented for each of the areas of occupational information discussed above: (a) occupational roles,

(b) occupational vocabulary, (c) occupational alternatives, and (d) basic information on some of the realities of the world of work.

Goals for Awareness of Occupational Roles

Primary Level (K-3)

Some important goals for young handicapped children during their primary grades are:

1. Students will demonstrate a knowledge of basic differences between the roles of paid and unpaid workers.
2. Students will demonstrate a knowledge of various worker roles that relate to differences in times for work and differences in amounts of time spent for work.
3. Students will demonstrate a knowledge of some of the basic worker role categories (indoor versus outdoor; rural versus urban; workers concerned with people, things, or ideas; etc.).
4. Students will verbalize, "I want to be a worker when I grow up — when can I start?"

Intermediate Level (4-6)

Some important goals for handicapped children during their intermediate grades are:

1. Students will demonstrate a knowledge of the two basic roles in the world of work — producer and consumer.
2. Students will demonstrate a knowledge of some examples of occupations characteristic of the roles of producers, consumers, maintainers, disposers, and recyclers.
3. Students will demonstrate a knowledge of worker roles by occupational clusters or primary service category.

4. Students will demonstrate a knowledge of the consumer role in the world of work by describing where various kinds of goods and services can be obtained.

Goals for Occupational Vocabulary

Primary Level (K-3)

Some appropriate goals for handicapped children during their first three or four school years follow. The first two objective statements are more appropriately taught in conjunction with specific occupations the children know or are learning. For example, coordinate them with the teaching of objective (3) below:

1. Students will demonstrate an understanding of the meaning of basic vocabulary related to various producer (worker) roles.
2. Students will demonstrate an understanding of the meaning of basic vocabulary related to various consumer roles.
3. Students will demonstrate an increase in their occupational vocabulary by being able to identify (by name) the occupations of all family members, all acquaintances in their neighborhood, and all workers in their school.

Intermediate Level (4-6)

Examples of goals for intermediate level handicapped children include:

1. Students will demonstrate a knowledge of the names of occupations within various selected occupational clusters.

2. Students will demonstrate an increase in their working occupational vocabulary by being able to identify (by name) workers in the community.
3. Students will demonstrate an increase in their working occupational vocabulary by being able to identify (by name) workers in the state and region.

Goals for Occupational Alternatives

Primary Level (K-3)

Some general goals for exceptional children at the primary level are:

1. Students will develop an identification with workers in various occupations.
2. Students will demonstrate knowledge of differences between occupational settings and roles.
3. Students will verbalize or communicate some initial choices of occupations.

Intermediate Level (4-6)

Representative goals for intermediate level handicapped children include:

1. Students will identify occupations that require the performance of activities they enjoy.
2. Students will explore interests that allow for wider choice among occupations or work roles.
3. Students will demonstrate an understanding that occupations and life styles are related.
4. Students will demonstrate continuing "choosing behaviors" among occupational alternatives to which they are exposed.

Goals for Basic Information
on Realities of the World of Work

Primary Level (K-3)

Some critical goals for handicapped children at the primary level include:

1. Students will demonstrate an understanding of the reality that most people in our society are engaged in some kind of work.
2. Students will demonstrate an understanding of the need for division of labor within the family, the classroom, and the community.
3. Students will demonstrate an understanding that work is a part of life and certain kinds of behaviors are expected when one is working.
4. Students will demonstrate an understanding that work nearly always involves someone telling someone else what to do, how to do it, and when to do it.
5. Students will demonstrate an understanding that people work for a number of reasons.

Intermediate Level (4-6)

Some important goals for intermediate level handicapped children are:

1. Students will demonstrate an awareness that although most people work, there are many people who cannot obtain work or who are not happy in the work they do.
2. Students will demonstrate an understanding of how the skills being learned at school relate to skills needed at work.
3. Students will demonstrate an understanding of the public nature of most work settings.
4. Students will demonstrate an awareness of the importance of time in work settings.

5. Students will demonstrate an understanding of the dependence and interdependence of workers and work settings.

6. Students will demonstrate an understanding of the existence of "unwritten rules" for workers on to how to act, how to talk, what to wear, etc.

7. Students will demonstrate a basic understanding of why some jobs pay more than other jobs.

8. Students will demonstrate an awareness that work, like play, can be monotonous or boring after doing it for a period of time, but that it is good to be able to be doing something of benefit for others or oneself.

With one exception, the goal statements presented above are stated in feasible pupil behavior outcomes. That is, children should be able to demonstrate their awareness, knowledge, or understanding to you by responding orally or in writing. The one exception is an experiential goal statement in which the behavior or outcome expected is the completion of an experience — without any need to respond in any way about that experience. Experiential objectives are legitimate, if used judiciously, and may be especially appropriate for particularly abstract concepts in career education. You may want to consider the use of experiential objectives for the components of attitudes, values, habits, and human relationships, as well as for occupational information. The important thing to remember is that an experiential objective essentially presents an activity or experience as being worthwhile in itself. This can be sorely abused if we set objectives that require no evaluation other than completion of the activity. This has led to the current emphasis on stating objectives in terms of *student* outcomes rather than teacher-planned activities for the pupils. Objectives without activities or experiences can be empty. To get to any point, you need to know both where you are going and how to get there. The following section gives some suggestions on "how to get there," with ideas on activities and materials to be used for instruction and guidance.

SELECTED ACTIVITIES AND MATERIALS FOR ACHIEVING GOAL/OBJECTIVE STATEMENTS

Of the three component areas of career education for the handicapped presented thus far, the area of occupational information has the greatest number of materials and activities resource books. This area has been infused into basic skill areas, particularly social studies, for some time. The emphasis on this area so far in the career education movement has also resulted in concentrated efforts toward curriculum material development. This section should give you a "starter" list of selected activities and materials that complement the examples of goal/objective statements discussed in this chapter.

Activities for Development of Occupational Information

Primary Level (K-3)

If you continue with the pattern suggested in previous chapters of moving instruction from self to environment, the familiar to the unfamiliar, and the concrete to the abstract, activities at the primary level should begin with and center upon the immediate environment — home and school. From this perspective, activities and experiences should be directed at opening vistas, stimulating fantasies, eliciting searching and questioning, and providing information to help children move beyond their immediate environments. Children at this age and educational level should respond to most of the following activities:

Occupational Roles and Alternatives
Interviewing parents and guardians about their jobs
Drawing pictures of parents or family members at work
Making worker puppets; putting on puppet worker "plays"
    and watching puppet role playing
Playing with adult hats, uniforms, or costumes

Engaging in semi-structured free play with a play store, play office, play clinic, play house, etc.

Making a wall mural of workers by categories or clusters of occupations.

Playing occupational jump rope (each pupil has a turn and calls out occupations while jumping; jumping continues until pupil misses or is unable to call out an occupation in rhythm)

Participating in structured dramatic play

Listening to parents, family members, and school workers who come to class and talk about their work

Reading picture and easy-to-read books (see Materials section)

Listening to songs or stories about workers (see Materials section)

Occupational Vocabulary

Career bingo (teacher-made boards with names of occupations)

Bulletin board focusing on occupational vocabulary

Occupational stimulus cards for visually identifying workers by name

Occupational sound stimulus tapes that auditorially identify workers by name

Lids for kids (pupils identify workers by caps, hats, or other headgear)

Occupational riddles

Occupational charades

Realities of the World of Work

Have parents assign children a work responsibility at home and complete a Home Worker's Checklist (see Appendix A)

Assign work responsibilities in the classroom and evaluate with a Classroom Worker's Checklist (see Appendix A)

Stories and easy-to-read books (see Materials section)

Films and filmstrips (see Materials section)

Class project using an assembly-line process

Intermediate Level (4-6)

In the intermediate grades, there can and should be an increase in the sophistication and realism of activities, without a loss of fun and interest. Students at this level may still enjoy pretending, but the props and the structure have to be much more realistic than at an earlier stage. Role playing, games, and simulation projects are popular at this level, along with field trips and "hands on" activities. Some examples include:

Occupational Roles and Alternatives
Group projects requiring role differentiation and division of labor, e.g., construction projects, newspapers, mini-restaurant or tea room, dramatic presentation, or musical show

Role playing based on new occupational information

Simulating a community to demonstrate dependence/interdependence of workers and work settings

Videotaping a process or sequence of services showing different worker roles

Teaching units on occupational clusters

Planning, writing, and filming a "documentary" on some occupation or cluster

Having community workers talk to the class about their work

Going on field trips to view or interview workers on the job

Conducting community surveys for community occupations

Conducting community surveys for volunteer work opportunities

Sponsoring exhibits by local businesses or industries

Sponsoring a school demonstration or exhibit by junior high school industrial arts classes and high school vocational education programs

Occupational Vocabulary
"What's My Line" (use television show game rules or adapt to meet abilities of pupils)

Occupational "Password" (use television show game rules but use only occupations as words)

Occupational crossword puzzles

Occupational games (see Materials section)

"Research" and report on new work roles

Realities of World of Work

Actual operation of a mini-business, e.g., school supply store, tea room, school bank, etc.

Work and work training simulation

Simulate a community or micro-society, demonstrating effects of economic variations ("booms" and recessions), labor strikes, natural disasters, etc.

Assign jobs in classroom or school and evaluate with a Classroom/School Worker Checklist (see Appendix A)

Rent-a-Kid Day (pupils work for an agreed-upon wage for a specific task on a given day)

Materials for Developing Occupational Information

Primary Level (K-3)

In addition to the limitless number of activities that could be used for teaching occupational information, there are some commercially available materials you should consider. Curricular materials, books, stories, audio-visual materials, games, and kits can help to introduce or develop accurate and pertinent occupational information. Some examples of these for each of the instructional levels follow.

1. *Stories and books:*
   Bangert, E. E. *Polly Perry, TV Cook* (Bertnam's, 1959).
   Beskov, E. *Pelle's New Suit* (Harper & Row, 1929).
   Butts, D. P. *The Story of Chocolate* (Steck-Vaughn, 1967).
   Colonius, L. *At the Bakery* (Melmont, 1967).
   Elkin, B. *True Book of Money* (Children's Press, 1960).

Fisher, L. E. *The Potters* (Watts, 1969).

Goldstein, H. *Identifying Helpers* (Merrill, 1974).

Kaufman, J. *Busy People* (Golden Press, 1973).

Klein, N. *Girls Can Be Anything* (Dutton, 1975).

Krayer, J. *Captain Kangaroo's Whole World Catalog* (Platt & Munk, 1976).

Lenski, L. *To Be a Logger* (Lippincott, 1967).

Lippman, P. *Busy Wheels* (Random House, 1973).

Moncure, J. B. *Jobs People Do* (Children's Press, 1976).

———— . *People Who Help People* (Children's Press, 1976).

Pickard, V. *Mr. Hobbs Can Fix It* (Hale, 1965).

Place, M. *Let's Go to a Fish Hatchery* (Putnam's, 1967).

Rosenbaum, E. *What Daddies Do* (Hallmark, 1970).

Russell, V. *Friendly Workers Visit Larry* (Denison, 1968).

Sacks, R. *Telephones* (Putnam's, 1965).

Scarry, R. *Busiest People Ever* (Random House, 1976).

———— . *Great Big Schoolhouse* (Random House, 1969).

———— . *What Do People Do All Day?* (Random House, 1968).

Wilcox, D. *I'm My Mommy/I'm My Daddy* (Western, 1975).

Williams, B. *I Know a Garageman* (Putnam's, 1968).

Young, M. *If I* Series (Lothrup, Lee & Shepard). *If I Drove a Bus* (1973). *If I Drove a Car* (1971). *If I Drove a Tractor* (1973). *If I Drove a Train* (1972). *If I Drove a Truck* (1967), *If I Flew a Plane* (1970), and *If I Sailed a Boat* (1971).

Ziegler, S. *At the Dentist: What Did Christopher See?* (Children's Press, 1977).

2. *Recordings (tapes, cassettes, or discs):*
   "Action Songs for Growing Up" (Children's Music Center).

   "Footnotes to Community Helpers: Grandpa Wiseman Tells" (H. Wilson Corporation).

   "Knowing Our Community Helpers" (School Speciality Supply, Inc.).

"Laundry and Bakery Story" (Folkways).

"Let's Be Firemen" (Young People's Records).

"Let's Be Policemen" (Young People's Records).

"My Mommy Is A Doctor" (Children's Book and Music Center).

"Our Working World" (Science Research Associates). Eight records which can be used independently or in conjunction with the SRA resource unit, *Neighbors at Work*.

"The Men Who Come To Our House" (Young People's Records).

3. *Films:*

"The Apple Industry" (Valiant Instructional Material Corporation).*

"Bus Driver" (Media Services and Captioned Films).

"City: Occupations" (Society for Visual Education).*

"The Dairy" (Valiant Instructional Material Corporation).*

The Kingdom of Could Be You Series (Encyclopaedia Britannica Educational Films).

Job Opportunities Series of Film Loops (Encyclopaedia Britannica Educational Films).*

The Real World Series (Centron Films). "Growing Up on the Farm Today," "Janie Sue and Tugaloo," "Jobs in the City: Distribution," "Jobs in the City: Construction," "Jobs in the City: Medical and Health," "Jobs in the City: Women at Work," "Jobs in the City: Mass Media," "Jobs in the City: Manufacturing," and "Jobs in the City: Services."

"What Ecologists Do" (Centron Films).

"What Shall I Be?" (Coronet).

"When You Grow Up" (AIMS Instructional Media Services).

When You Grow Up Series (Mini Productions).

"Who's Who in the Zoo?" (Centron Films).

---

*Super 8mm silent color filmloops.

4. *Filmstrips:*
   "America at Work" (Eye Gate).
   "Our Neighborhood Workers" (Eye Gate).
   "People Who Work While You Sleep" (Popular Science).
   "Some Neighborhood Helpers" (Eye Gate).
5. *Television programs and videotapes:*
   Captain Kangaroo's *The Kingdom of Could Be You Series* (Columbia Broadcasting System). See also Film section for availability in 16mm films.
   "Freestyle" (Public Broadcasting Service).
   "Sesame Street" (Public Broadcasting Service).
   Vegetable Soup Series (New York State Board of Education). Twenty-six minidocumentaries with teacher's guide.
6. *Songs*
   Action Songs for Growing Up (Children's Music Center).
   I Wonder What I'll Be (Shawnee Press).
   Music for Young Americans: Discovering Music — 2 (American Book Company).
   Music Round the Town (Follett Publishing Company).
   This Is Music, volumes 2 and 5 (Allyn & Bacon).
   Note: There are numerous individual songs in these music books for appropriate selections.

7. *Manipulative toys or games:*
   "Friends" (Western Publishing Company).
   "Helpers Three-In-One Game" (Educational Achievement Corporation).
   "Occupation Series of Wooden Puzzles" (General Learning Corporation).
   Valuing Game Series (Educational Achievement Corporation).
   "When I Grow Up I Want To Be" (Instructo Corporation).
   "Working People Games" (New Dimensions in Education, Inc.).

8. *Multimedia kits:*

Career Awareness Series (Educational Activities, Inc.). Sound filmstrips. "School," "Hospital," "Airport," and "Construction Workers."

Career Development for Children Project (McKnight). Level I: "Discovering Self in Work and Play," Level II: "Exploring Interests in Work and Play," and Level III: "Using Knowledge in the World of Work."

Career Kits for Kids Series (Encyclopaedia Britannica, Inc.). Sound filmstrips, posters, worker hats, spirit masters, and teacher's guide. "Barney the Baker," "Freddy the Fireman," "Maxi the Taxi Driver," "Nellie the Nurse," and "Rusty the Construction Worker."

Community Workers and Helpers Series, Group I (Society for Visual Education). Five sound filmstrips with teacher's guide.

OIDMA *General Awareness Series* (OIDMA, Ltd.). Sound filmstrips.

OIDMA *Specific Career Awareness Series* (OIDMA, Ltd.). Two series comprised of ten sound filmstrips each.

Our Working World Series (Science Research Associates). Records, scriptbook for teacher, resource unit with suggested activities, stories, poems, etc. "Families at Work," "Neighborhoods at Work," and "Cities at Work."

People Who Work Series (Scholastic). Sound filmstrips, cardboard job hats, paper finger puppets, and teacher's guide. Unit 1: "Say Ah," "Bake a Batch," "Park Ranger," "Stitch 'n Stuff," and "Pick a Pattern, Pick a Patch." Unit 2: "Follow the Architect's Plan," "Click," "Jet Pilot," "Pets for Sale," and "On Rainbow Farm."

Programmed Work Awareness Kit (Chronicle Guidance Publications). Thirty weekly instructional units with picture charts, picture cards, games, records, cash register, coins, puppets, pupil activity books, and teacher's guide.

Real People at Work Series "Instruction Kit K-2" (Changing Times Education Service Inc.). Activity sheets, posters, records, "helper" badges, bulletin board display, spirit masters, and teacher's guide.

The Very Important People Series (Children's Press). Cassette sound filmstrips, student involvement sheets, and teacher's guide.

Wally, the Worker Watcher Series (Denoyer-Geppert). Eleven sound filmstrips in cartoon format.

What Does Your Dad Do? Series (Scott Education Division). Sound filmstrips.

Working in the World Series (Clearvue, Inc.). Filmstrips with cassette or records and teacher's guide. "The Farm is for Me," "A Factory Hums Along," "A Hospital Helps People," "School Days," "Everybody Eats," and "Trucks, Boats, and Planes."

9. *Miscellaneous:*

A Highway to Work and Play (McKnight). Leaflets with teacher's guide. Level 1: "Getting Started," Level 2: "Moving On," and Level 3: "Traveling Together."

Career Flash Cards (BFA Educational Media). Pupil and teacher flash cards.

"People Who Help Our Community" (Troll Associates). Ten color transparencies.

Transparency Kit (Education Service Center). Forty transparencies and teacher's guide.

"When I Grow Up, I Want to Be . . ." (Instructo Corporation). Flannel board dolls and worker costumes.

"When You Grow Up: Study Posters for Elementary Career Awareness" (Mini Production). Fifteen posters.

Intermediate Level (4-6)

Instructional activities and materials for teaching occupational information should be advanced enough to provide more information to students about their role as workers now and in the future so that more and more realism can be observed in their behavior. On the other hand, the materials and instructional activities should remain concrete enough to keep the students "plugged in" to the idea that "There are lots of opportunities to be a productive person and some of them I can do." The commercial materials may or may not be entirely appropriate at the designated grade levels for mentally or educationally handicapped students. Materials should also be carefully evaluated for sexual or racial stereotyping because children at this age level are mature enough to begin to think in terms of these factors.

The intermediate level is typically the level at which students begin to use their reading, writing, and oral communication skills to acquire information more rapidly and independently. Many language arts, social studies, math, and science materials can be related to occupational information, and infusion of all career education concepts is more feasible at this level. Field trips, visiting speakers, films, recordings, simulated activities, and games are especially appropriate for intermediate children. Keep in mind that many handicapped children will not be skilled in reading, writing, and oral discussions and these activities should be used only when the activities are well within their performance level. Fortunately, many of the materials currently being developed for career education programming use multisensory approaches that minimize reading as the prime information receptor. The following materials are examples of available materials for the intermediate level:

1. *Stories and books:*
   Armstrong, L. *How to Turn Lemons Into Money* (Harcourt, Brace, & Jovanovich, 1976).

   Benson, C. *An Early Career Book Series* (Lerner, 1976). *Careers in Agriculture, Careers in Auto Sales and Service, Careers in Conservation,* and *Careers with the City.*

Baker, E. *I Want to Be Books* (Children's Press). *I Want to Be — An Auto Mechanic, A Draftsman, A Gymnast, A Postal Clerk, A Soccer Player, A Travel Agent, A Bank Teller, A Computer Operator, A Secretary, A Waitress, A Forester, A Service Station Attendant, A Taxi Driver, An Architect, A Lawyer, A Weatherman, A Football Player, A Hockey Player, A Swimmer, A Beauty Operator, A Jeweler, A Printer,* or *A Telephone Operator.*

Berger, G. *Jobs that Help the Consumer and the Homemaker* (Lothrup, Lee, and Shepard, 1977).

————. *Jobs that Save Our Environment* (Lothrup, Lee, and Shepard, 1973).

Chilton, S., and Chilton, R. *Everyone Has Important Jobs to Do* (Children's Press, 1970).

Criner, B., and Criner, C. *Jobs in Personal Services* (Lothrup, Lee, and Shepard, 1974).

Dobrin, A. *Jobs in Recreation* (Lothrup, Lee, and Shepard, 1974).

Englebardt, S. L. *Jobs in Health Care* (Lothrup, Lee, and Shepard, 1973).

Felder, E. *Careers in Publishing and Printing* (Raintree, 1977).

Fenton, D. X. *TV and Radio Careers* (Franklin Watts, 1976).

Fiorotta, P., and Fiorotta, N. *Be What You Want to Be!* (Workman, 1977).

Freeman, D. R., Westover, M., and Willis, W. *The Very Important Person Series* (Children's Press). Set 1: *The Work World of Wheels* (1973), Set 2: *The Work World of Health* (1973), Set 3: *The Work World of Communication* (1975), and Set 4: *The Work World of Personal Services* (1976).

Goldreich, G., and Goldreich, E. *What Can She Be Series* (Lothrup, Lee, and Shepard). *What Can She Be? — An Architect* (1974), *A Farmer* (1976), *A Geologist* (1976), *A Lawyer* (1973), *A Musician* (1975),

A *Newscaster* (1973), *A Police Officer* (1975), or *A
Veterinarian* (1972).

Horn, Y. M. *Dozens of Ways to Make Money* (Harcourt,
Brace, & Jovanovich, 1977).

Johnston, J. *Women Themselves* (Dodd, 1973).

Liebers, A. *You Can Be Series* (Lothrup, Lee, and
Shepard). *You Can Be — A Carpenter* (1973), *An
Electrician* (1974), *A Machinist* (1975), *A Mechanic*
(1975), *A Plumber* (1974), *A Printer* (1976), *A Professional Driver* (1976).

Mathieu, J. *Big Joe's Trailer Truck* (Random House,
1974).

Paulsen, G. *Careers in an Airport* (Raintree, 1977).

Powell, M., and Yokubinas, G. *What To Be?* (Children's
Press, 1972).

Schaleben-Lewis, J. *Careers in a Supermarket* (Raintree,
1977).

————. *Careers in a Hospital* (Raintee, 1976).

Stanhope, L. *Careers in a Department Store* (Raintree,
1976).

Wakin, E. *Jobs in Communication* (Lothrup, Lee, and
Shepard, 1974).

2. *Recordings (tapes, cassettes, or discs):*
What's It Like? Cassette Tape Series (Knowledge Aid).
Twenty-two cassette tape interviews made especially
for students from ethnic minority groups.

3. *Films:*
"A City Awakens" (Churchill Films).
"Anything They Want to Be." (Extension Media Cen-
ter).
Bread and Butterflies Series (Agency for Instructional
Television). "Choosing Changes," "Decisions, Deci-
sions," "I Agree . . . You're Wrong!," "Me, Myself,
and Maybe," "Our Own Two Hands," "People Need
People," "Planning Ahead: The Racer," "Power
Play," "School and Jobs," "Success Story," "Taking
Care of Business," "The Way We Live," "Things,

Ideas, People," "Treasure Hunt," and "Work Means . . ."
"Building A Skyscraper and the Careers Involved" (AIMS Instructional Media Services, Inc.).
"Careers in a Large Industry" (Vocational Films).
Economics Geography Series (Centron Films). "Beef: The Steak in the Grass," "Coal: The Rock that Burns," "Corn: The Plant with Ears," "Dairy Products: From Moo to You," "Oil: From Fossil to Flame," "Peanuts: And the Peanut Butter Plant," "Poultry: Laying It On The Line," "Soybeans: The Magic Beanstalk," and "Wheat: From Field to Flour."
"Firefighter" (Aspect IV Educational Films Company).
"Hospital Careers" (Oxford Films, Inc.).
Job Opportunities Series of Film Loops (Encyclopaedia Britannica Educational Films).*
"Lumber Mills" (Valiant Instructional Materials Corporation).*
"Mr. Busboy" (Media Services and Captioned Films).
"The Mailmen" (Media Services and Captioned Films).
People Who Work (Churchill Films).
The Real World Series (Centron Films). See film section for primary level for series titles.
Whatcha Gonna Do Series (Encyclopaedia Britannica Educational Films).
"What Ecologists Do" (Centron Films).
When I Grow Up Series (ACI Productions). "I Can Be a Builder," "I Can Be a Community Service Worker," "I Can Be a Food Processing Worker," "I Can Be a Hospital Worker," or "I Can Be a Mechanic."
"When You Grow Up" (AIMS Instructional Media Services).
When You Grow Up Series (Counselor Films, Inc.). "Business: Pet Store," "Communication: Television," "Construction," "Health," and "Natural Resources Park Ranger."
"Who's Who in the Zoo?" (Centron Films).

*Super 8mm silent color filmloops.

4. *Filmstrips:*
   "Fathers Work" (Roberts Audio Visual Learning Arts).
   "Mothers Work, Too" (School Speciality Supply, Inc.).
   "Systems In-Out City: Community Series" (McGraw-Hill Films).
   "The American Farmer and Our Food Supply" (Eye Gate House, Inc.).
   "The Wonderful World of Work" (Denoyer-Geppert).
   "The World of Work — Vocational Opportunities" (Eye Gate House, Inc.).
   "Who Works For You?" (Random House).

5. *Television and videotapes:*
   Bread and Butterflies Series (Agency for Instructional Television). See series titles under film section.
   "Freestyle" (Public Broadcasting Service).

6. *Songs:*
   Music for Young Americans Song Book (American Book Company).
   Music In Our Country (Silver Burdett Company).
   New Music Horizons Song Book (Silver Burdett Company).
   Singing Together (Ginn & Company).
   We Stand Together (Listener Educational Enterprises, Inc.).
   Note: These music books contain some appropriate song selections for intermediate level.

7. *Games:*
   "Career Insights and Self Awareness Games" (Houghton Mifflin).
   "Careers" (Parker Brothers).
   "Expo 10: Exploring Career Interests" (Science Research Associates).
   "Our Helpers" (Milton Bradley Company).
   "Pay Day" (Parker Brothers).
   "Steady Job" (Mafex Associates, Inc.).
   "The Fortune Fun Game" (Educational Achievement Corporation).

"Worker Charades Game" (Educational Achievement Corporation).

8. *Multimedia kits:*
   Adventures in the World of Work (Random House). Books, filmstrips, spirit masters, and teacher's guide. *Note:* Books and filmstrips can be used together or independently.
   "Artist at Work" (Jim Handy Company). Five sound color filmstrips.
   Career Awareness Filmstrips (Childcraft). Sound filmstrips, student activity book, and teacher's manual. "I Have A Body," "I Have A Brain," "The Work People Do," "I Can Do Things," and "I Can Make Choices."
   Career Awareness Program (King Features) Booklets with Popeye cartoon format, Career Awareness Bingo game, student involvement posters, display and storage rack, and teacher's guide.
   "Career Mothers" (Audiovisual Instructional Devices). Six sound filmstrips.
   Careers: A Supplemental Reading Program (Harcourt, Brace, Jovanovich, Inc.). Three grade level (4-6) kits containing sound filmstrips, story folders, posters, activity cards, student management folders, and teacher's guide.
   Community Workers and Helpers Series, Group II (Society for Visual Education). Five sound filmstrips.
   Compulearn Career Education Program (Random House). Battery operated console, 142 compulearn guide, and instructional guide.
   Explore (Scholastic). Records or cassettes with print materials. Unit 1: "Work? Play?," Unit 2: "Who? What? When? Why?," Unit 3: "Career Connections."
   Lerner Early Career Books (Lerner Publications) Student textbooks, study prints, and teaching guide.
   Our Community Utilities (Coronet). Four color sound filmstrips. "Electricity," "Gas," "The Telephone," "Water."

Our Working World Series (Science Research Associates). Records, scriptbook for teachers, and resource unit with suggested activities, stories, poems, etc. "Regions of the United States" and "The American Way of Life."

"People at Work" (Pathescope). Thirty sound filmstrips, spirit masters, and teacher's guide. *Note:* This kit has a Spanish version of some of the units; contact publisher for an up-to-date listing.

Random House Career Awareness Program (Random House). Sound filmstrips, spirit masters, and teacher's guide. "Adventures in the World of Work," and "Who Works for You?"

Real People at Work Series: Instructional Kits 3-5 (Changing Times Education Service, Inc.). Books, read-along cassettes, activity sheets, posters, bulletin board display, spirit masters, and teacher's guide.

Real People at Work Series: Sound Filmstrip Program (Changing Times Education Service, Inc.). Sound filmstrips and teacher's guide. "Careers and Concepts in Industry," "From Classroom to Career," and "The Economy: How It Works."

The Scott Education Career Awareness Program (Scott Education Division). Sound filmstrips, unit overviews (8), and teacher's guide.

"The American Farmer and Our Food Supply" (Eye Gate House, Inc.). Nine sound color filmstrips.

"We Stand Together" (Listener Educational Enterprises, Inc.). Fourteen audio cassettes, posters, games, lyric sheets, booklet, and teacher's guide.

9. *Miscellaneous:*

"A Highway to Work and Play" (McKnight). Leaflets with teacher's guide. Level 4: "Changing Signals," nals," Level 5: "Making Decisions," Level 6: "Turning Points."

Career Concepts, Series 1 (Science Research Associates). Structured instructional unit.

Career World 1 (Curriculum Innovations, Inc.). Career development magazine for grades 4-6.

"What Could I Be?" (Science Research Associates). Pupil textbooks and teacher's guide.

REFERENCES

Barnett, R. C., and Baruch, G. Occupational and educational aspirations and expectations: A review of empirical literature. Unpublished manuscript, 1973.

Baumrind, D. From each according to her ability. *School Review* 80 (1972): 161-197.

Bell, D. *Work and its discontents.* Boston: Beacon Press, 1956.

Boyd, F. F. The levels and aspirations of white and negro children in a nonsegregated elementary school. *Journal of Social Psychology* 36 (1952): 191-196.

Boynton, P. The vocational preferences of school children. *Journal of Genetic Psychology* 49 (1936): 411-425.

Clark, E. T. Influence of sex and social class on occupational preference and perception. *Personnel and Guidance Journal* 45 (1967): 440-444.

Clark, G. M. Career education for the mildly handicapped. *Focus on Exceptional Children* 5 (9) (1974): 1-10.

Crooks, R. C. The effects of an interracial preschool program upon racial preference, knowledge of racial differences, and racial identification. *Journal of Social Issues* 27 (1971): 213-235.

Crowne, D. P., and Stephens, M. W. Self acceptance and self-evaluation behavior: A critique of methodology. *Psychological Bulletin* 58 (1961): 104-121.

Deutsch, M. Minority group and class status as related to social and personality factors in scholastic achievement. *Monographs of the Society for Applied Anthropology*, No. 2, 1960.

Englander, M. A psychological analysis of vocational choice: Teaching. *Journal of Consulting Psychology* 7 (1960): 257-264.

Farber, B. *Mental retardation: Its social context and social consequences.* Boston: Houghton Mifflin, 1968.

Ginzberg, E., Ginsburg, S. W., Axelrad, S., and Herma, J. L. *Occupational information: An approach to a general theory.* New York: Columbia University Press, 1951.

Goodman, P. Youth in organized society. *Commentary* 29 (1960): 95-107.

Henrich, E., and Kriegel, L. *Experiments in survival.* New York: Foundation for Child Development (formerly the Association for the Aid of Crippled Children), 1961.

Hodge, R. W., Siegel, P. M., and Rossi, P. H. Occupational prestige in the United States, 1925-1963. *American Journal of Sociology* 72 (1966): 286-295.

Hoyt, K. B. *An introduction to career education.* Policy paper of the U.S. Office of Education, DHEW Publications No. (OE)75-00504. Washington, D.C.: U.S. Government Printing Office, 1975.

―――― . *Career education and the handicapped person.* Unpublished address, U.S. Office of Education, Washington, D.C., no date.

Lee, P. C., and Gropper, N. B. Sex-role culture and educational practice. *Harvard Educational Review* 44 (1974): 369-410.

Leifer, A. D., and Lesser, G. S. *The development of career awareness in young children.* NIE Papers in Education and Work: No. 1. Washington, D.C.: National Institute of Education, 1976.

Lipsett, L. Social factors in vocational development. *Personnel and Guidance Journal* 40 (1962): 432-437.

Looft, W. R. Sex differences in the expression of vocational aspirations by elementary school children. *Developmental Psychology* 5 (1971): 366.

Maccoby, E. E., and Jacklin, C. N. *The psychology of sex differences.* Stanford, California: Stanford University Press, 1974.

Maslow, A. H. *Motivation and personality.* New York: Harper and Row, 1954.

Miller, D. C., and Form, W. H. *Industrial sociology.* New York: Harper and Brothers, 1951.

Neff, W. S. *Work and human behavior.* New York: Atherton Press, 1968.

Nelson, J. C. Interests of disadvantaged negro and white first graders. *Journal of Negro Education* 37 (1968): 168-173.

Riesman, D., with D. Reuel and N. Glazer. *The lonely crowd.* New Haven, Connecticut: Yale University Press, 1950.

Schlossberg, N. K., and Goodman, J. A. A woman's place: Children's sex stereotypes of occupations. *Vocational Guidance Quarterly* 20 (1972): 266-270.

Siegel, C. L. F. Sex differences in the occupational choices of second graders. *Journal of Vocational Behavior* 3 (1973): 15-19.

Super, D. E. *Career development: Self concept theory.* New York: The College Entrance Examination Board, Teachers College, Columbia University, 1963.

―――― . Vocational adjustment: Implementing a self concept. *Occupations* 30 (1951): 88-91.

Sutton-Smith, B. *The folkgames of children.* Austin, Texas: University of Texas Press, 1972.

Terkel, S. *Working.* New York: Avon, 1975.

Weagraff, P. J. Career education curriculum development using the cluster concept. *Educational Horizons* 51 (1973): 149-156.

Whyte, W. H. *The organization man.* New York: Simon & Schuster, 1956.

Wylie, R. C. Children's estimates of their schoolwork ability as a function of sex, race, and socio-economic level. *Journal of Personality* 31 (1963): 203-224.

―――― . *The self concept.* Lincoln, Nebraska: University of Nebraska Press, 1961.

5

CAREER EDUCATION PROGRAMMING FOR ACQUISITION OF JOB AND DAILY LIVING SKILLS

By now the broad needs of the handicapped in career education should be obvious. There is equally strong logic and data available to argue for similar programming for non-handicapped persons as well. The model presented here should have relevance for any group of children for whom the overall goals of education in general and career education in particular are not being accomplished.

My model is based on the notion that career education must focus on the totality of a person's competencies if "career" is going to be defined in its most generic sense as "a person's course or progress through life" (Oxford English Dictionary, 1961). A person can have "good" attitudes, values, and habits but still be considered incompetent in personal or work behaviors. A person can be adept in human relationships but still be judged as unskilled in occupational or daily living tasks. A person can have knowledge about the world of work but be unable to maintain a place in it without skills in job or personal-social behavior requirements. This being the case, it seems only natural that the acquisition of job and daily living skills be made a mutually important element of the model.

The literature in career education currently available focuses on occupational awareness, exploration, and preparation. Whatever mention is made of attitudes, values, and habits is usually directly related to the goals of developing positive attitudes, values, and habits toward work in paid employment. Similarly, whatever mention is made of human relationships usually ties in with social interactions on the job. The importance of competence in daily living and how daily living skills relate to success in the world of work are rarely mentioned. Daily living skills must receive emphasis equal to job skills if students are to be fully equipped to deal with life.

Actually, job skills and daily living skills overlap in so many instances that there should be little need to debate the necessity of including daily living skills in a curriculum model. The skills required for reading a recipe to cook a meal at home are the same as those needed for reading a recipe for a restaurant cooking job. The skills required for driving a car or truck for personal reasons are the skills required for driving a car or truck in a work setting. The skills needed for selecting and purchasing items for personal use are basically the same skills required for selecting and buying goods in the work world.

There are, obviously, scores of daily living demands that require skills or competencies not associated directly with occupational skills. These skills are still justifiable within a career education context because they are critical competencies that undergird all experiences of life. Failure to acquire competencies in daily living cannot be isolated from one's success or failure in the world of work. This has been demonstrated time and again in the case of handicapped adults. Recent studies have shown that inadequate daily living skills hamper 20 percent of all nonhandicapped adults in the United States as well (New Readers Press News, 1977). If a person cannot maintain a healthy body, how can he or she work? If a person cannot abide by the laws of a community or state, how can he or she be expected to abide by the laws or rules of the work world? If a person does not know how to use leisure time at home, how can he or she be expected to use a work break effectively? If a person has marital or family relationship problems, how can he or she be expected to work up to full performance potential?

De Grazia (1962) suggests another way of looking at the myriad skills and competencies not directly related to occupational skills. He contends that the important elements of life can be viewed from a perspective of time, and categorizes time spent in the following ways:

Work: paid employment

Subsistence: eating, sleeping, being under medical care, basic grooming, cooking, shopping, etc.

Free time: any time spent without obligations, frequently in recreation, entertainment, hobbies, walks, etc.

All the rest: going to dentist, getting the car repaired, voting, writing business letters, going to barber or beautician, attending P.T.A., taking children to music lessons, etc.

From this point of view, innumerable competencies or skills are needed to function in the time not spent at work.

It has already been noted that elementary aged children do experience work roles and are capable of performing simple to fairly complex tasks. Any job performance, occupational, or daily living skill requires one or more basic skills. They are typically categorized under cognitive skills, affective skills, and psychomotor skills. Affective skills were discussed at length in chapters 2 and 3. In this chapter we will focus on the specific programming in basic cognitive and psychomotor skills children with mental or physical handicaps should have to (a) prepare them for current and emerging work roles during childhood, (b) prepare them for assuming more complex work roles during adolescence, (c) prepare them for coping with current and emerging daily living demands, and to (d) prepare them for coping with the more complex demands to be made on them in daily living during adolescence. Figure 5.1 gives examples of basic skills that would be appropriate for each of the four preparation areas.

Although Figure 5.1 is an oversimplification of the scope and sequence desirable for programming in job and daily living skills, it can serve as a guide for curriculum planning. Many skills it mentions are already taught in the elementary school on a formal, systematic basis, and you might question the inclusion of such traditional skill areas as reading, spelling, and mathematics in a plan for acquiring job and daily living skills. Without apology, I suggest that all learners should be taught to perceive learning as useful to themselves and to society. Marland (1974, p. 13) quotes Alfred North Whitehead as saying: "Pedants sneer at an education that is useful. But if it is not useful, what is it?" For whatever reasons, we educators have too frequently lost sight of this basic proposition in designing our curricula and organizing our schools. Thus, if *learners* are to perceive learning as useful, *you* must as well, and you must communicate clearly *how* it can be useful.

What a child who is handicapped perceives as useful now or in the future may differ from your perception as an elementary educator. This is one of the dangers of deciding what is useful on the basis of necessary adult competencies. They often seem too far removed, though they are really not. Brolin (1974) has formulated twenty-two basic competencies needed for career adjustment by the educable mentally retarded. They are so generic, however, that they would be perceived by most people as minimal competencies for anyone. Because of their general comprehensiveness, they are presented below as examples of curriculum content that undeniably reflect "usefulness":

1. Managing family finances;
2. Caring for home furnishings and equipment;
3. Caring for personal needs;
4. Rearing children, family living;
5. Buying and preparing food;

Preparation Areas	Cognitive Skills	Psychomotor Skills
Preparation for current/emerging work roles	Reading Knowledge of safety Memory	Eye-hand coordination (cleaning chalkboard, sweeping, etc.) Finger dexterity (cutting with scissors, pasting, small parts assembly, etc.)
Preparation for assuming more complex work roles	Vocabulary Spelling Basic math facts Problem-solving	Manual dexterity (balancing, stacking, materials handling, etc.) Strength (lifting, pulling, pushing, etc.) Stamina
Preparation for current/emerging daily living demands	Semi-independent travel and mobility Semi-independent self care Semi-independent use of money	Eye-hand coordination (combing hair, sewing on button, etc.) Finger dexterity (peeling an apple, trimming fingernails, etc.)
Preparation for coping with more complex daily living demands	Decision making Independent travel Independent self-care	Manual dexterity (shoe shining, hair rolling, etc.) Eye-hand-motor coordination (driving, home repairs, cooking, etc.)

Figure 5.1. Basic skills for job and daily living preparation.

6. Buying and making clothing;
7. Engaging in civic activities;
8. Utilizing recreation and leisure;
9. Being mobile in the community;
10. Achieving self-awareness;
11. Acquiring self-confidence;
12. Achieving socially responsive behavior;
13. Maintaining good interpersonal skills;
14. Achieving independence;
15. Making good decisions, problem-solving;
16. Communicating adequately with others;
17. Knowing and exploring occupational possibilities;
18. Making appropriate occupational decisions;
19. Exhibiting appropriate work behaviors;
20. Exhibiting adequate physical and manual skills;
21. Acquiring a specific saleable job skill; and
22. Seeking, securing, and maintaining satisfactory employment.

We can consider competencies 1 through 19 as examples of daily living skills and competencies 20 and 21 as related to job skills. Using these as starting points, we will transform their usefulness for adult living to usefulness for elementary children with handicaps.

For example, competency #1 is *managing family finances.* In teaching basic coin recognition skills, primary grade children should not be told that they need to learn to name and identify pennies, nickels, and dimes because they will need that knowledge to be able to identify quarters and half dollars later on, or because someday they will be responsible for managing their family finances. Both reasons may be valid, but they are not reasons that will appear useful to the children. They are much more likely to perceive coin identification as a meaningful task if it is presented in a problem-solving situation in which their ability to differentiate among the coins determines whether they have one penny to spend or one quarter. *That* is useful! Bereiter (1974) speaks to this very point in a book called *Conflicting Conceptions of Curriculum:*

> It is almost unbelievable that intelligent school children could take so long to learn so few computation skills so poorly as they do in our elementary schools, especially when you consider that street children in poor countries learn money arithmetic unerringly at an age when an American child cannot be trusted to add three and three. (p. 24)

Perhaps it would be helpful to use the Brolin (1974) competencies as a framework for clarifying the nature and importance of daily living and job skills development at the elementary level. The brief descriptions of each competency that follow focus on some of the critical useful skills elementary-aged handicapped children should acquire:

Managing family finances. Children at the elementary level should acquire the basic skills of managing their own money. These skills comprise what is typically proposed for elementary consumer education. Some examples of management skills include: (a) coin and paper money recognition, (b) counting with money, (c) safe accumulation and deposit in a home or community bank, and (d) saving to buy a specific item.

Caring for home furnishings and equipment. Children should acquire basic skills in (a) dusting and polishing wood furniture, (b) vacuuming or dusting rugs, mats, or carpets, (c) cleaning mirrors, windows, and glass doors, and (d) simple repairs or item replacement (tightening screws, replacing furnace filters, replacing light bulbs, etc.).

Caring for personal needs. Children at this level should be able to demonstrate skill in (a) personal grooming, (b) home and school safety, (c) personal hygiene, and (d) basic health and nutrition.

Rearing children; family living. At this level, children should be able to (a) assist in or assume full responsibility for the care of a pet, (b) assume responsibility for a younger child in a play or learning situation for a short period of time, and (c) demonstrate skill in contacting key emergency personnel, such as physicians, policemen, firemen, and building superintendents.

Buying and preparing food. Elementary children should have skills in (a) making basic food purchases, (b) preparing their own snacks, (c) preparing their own meals (soup, sandwich, warm "leftovers," etc.) in the absence of an adult or older brother or sister, and (d) assisting in the preparation of a complete meal.

Buying and making clothing. Skills in this competency may vary according to opportunities at home, but most children should be able to (a) assist in making appropriate selections in clothes according to size, seasonal requirements, durability, and appearance, and (b) make simple purchases of clothing, such as socks, caps, mittens, and T-shirts.

Engaging in civic activities. Handicapped children can feel more a part of the community if they have acquired skills in (a) participating in community events, (b) complying with community customs, traditions, and laws, and (c) initiating appropriate actions to help keep the community clean and safe.

Utilizing recreation and leisure. Elementary-aged handicapped children should be able to (a) plan recreation or free play activities and follow through with them for a specific block of leisure time, (b) use home entertainment devices (television set, radio, record player, etc.) appropriately and independently, (c) participate in a group recreation activity, and (d) use at least one community recreation facility appropriately.

Being mobile in the community. Children with handicaps may find this competency particularly difficult but should still be able to demonstrate skills in (a) orientation to neighborhood and community to prevent getting lost, (b) use of at least one community transit system, and (c) independent travel in the neighborhood as a pedestrian.

Exhibiting sufficient physical and manual skills. To the extent that they are physically able to perform independently or with the aid of a prosthesis, elementary handicapped children should be able to demonstrate skills in (a) gross motor activities (standing, walking, running), (b) handling body weight in strength, speed, and coordination, (c) motor coordination (lifting, carrying, pushing, pulling, hammering, tossing, catching), and (d) fine motor activities (pincer grasp, twisting, turning, reaching, grasping, and use of small hand tools).

Acquiring specific saleable job skills. Once again, to the extent that they are physically able to perform independently or with the aid of a prosthesis, specialized tool or equipment, or jig, the elementary handicapped child should be able to demonstrate skills in (a) cleaning (sweeping, mopping, polishing, etc.), (b) selling (minimal skills in taking orders, making change, or using a cash register), (c) providing personal services (delivering messages, running errands, providing lawn care, baby sitting, etc.), (d) basic communication (reading, speaking, and writing), and (e) basic number concepts and arithmetic facts.

Job and daily living skills are not just important for their usefulness; they are also important because our society expects everyone to be able to demonstrate these kinds of competencies. There are certain social "penalties" the handicapped have to pay if they cannot perform them — stares, comments, embarrassed interactions and well-meant but ignorant questions are typical. Competence in as many skills as possible helps the handicapped present themselves as more like the nonhandicapped; more "normal."

Adjustment to everyday life in our society is dependent upon the mastery of a large number of relatively simple, repetitive acts that are part of the normal rhythm of a day. They include rising to some type of call or alarm, getting dressed, participating in play or work activities, taking care of one's needs, pursuing interests, responsibilities, or concerns, and going to bed. The importance of learning to perform such acts relates to the normalization principle, which holds that the handicapped should be provided with "means which are as culturally normative as possible in order to establish and/or maintain behaviors and characteristics which are as culturally normative as possible" (Wolfensberger, 1972, p. 28). A career education curriculum should serve as the "means" to that desired end.

Your approach to instructional planning in this area should be based on an acceptance of the normalization principle and employ some formalized assumptions to provide direction in planning. The assumptions which follow are founded on the general programmatic assumptions for career education presented in *An Introduction to Career Education* (Hoyt, 1975):

1. Basic academic, psychomotor, and daily living skills are survival and adaptability tools needed by the handicapped in today's rapidly changing society.
2. Increasingly, entry into today's work world demands that those who seek employment possess a specific set of occupational skills.
3. A positive relationship exists between education and level of occupational attainment, but the amount and kind of education required for competence at any level varies greatly from occupation to occupation and from life style to life style.
4. Academic, psychomotor, and daily living skills can be taught to and learned by most people. Individuals can effectively use such skills to enhance their career development.
5. Daily living skills are inextricably interwoven with the process of working and may be as significantly involved in success or failure for the handicapped as occupational skills.
6. Although daily living skills are often considered the primary responsibility of the family, the school must assume a greater and more systematic responsibility in instructional programming in this area for handicapped pupils.
7. Many routine daily living skills can be taught for predictable situations; others become obsolete because of our changing environment and technology. Consequently, problem-solving and decision-making skills should be taught as process skills.

The following section presents a series of representative goal or objective statements for daily living and job skill acquisition. The final section suggests activities and materials related to the goal statements and to skill acquisition in general.

SELECTED GOAL/OBJECTIVE STATEMENTS

The following examples of goal or objective statements are separated according to daily living skills and job skills at the primary and intermediate grade levels.

Goals for Acquisition of Daily Living Skills

Primary Level (K-3)

Examples of important goals for young handicapped children during their primary grades are:

1. Students will demonstrate skills in using simulated or real money.
2. Students will demonstrate skills in caring for school furnishings and equipment.
3. Students will demonstrate skills in independent self-care in grooming and personal hygiene.
4. Students will demonstrate skills in participating in community events.
5. Students will demonstrate skills in using a television set, a radio, and a record player.
6. Students will demonstrate skill in finding their way back to school from a point in the immediate neighborhood.

Intermediate Level (4-6)

Some examples of important goals for handicapped children at this level are:

1. Students will demonstrate skills in saving to buy a specific item.
2. Students will demonstrate skills in school and home safety.

127

3. Students will demonstrate skills in specific care techniques for wooden furniture, vinyl covered surfaces, glass surfaces, and rugs.
4. Students will demonstrate skills in accepting responsibility for a younger child in a play or learning situation for a reasonable, but prescribed, period of time.
5. Students will demonstrate skills in selecting and buying (simulated or real) appropriate clothes for school and play.
6. Students will demonstrate skills in detecting and responding to neighborhood ecology problems.
7. Students will demonstrate skills in using a community recreation or entertainment facility.
8. Students will demonstrate skill in using at least one community transit system (real or simulated), such as a taxi, bus, or subway.

Goals for Acquisition of Job Skills

Primary Level (K-3)

Some representative goals for handicapped children in the area of job skills include:

1. Students will demonstrate skills in basic gross motor activities (walking, running, bending, and jumping).
2. Students will demonstrate skills in balance and coordination.
3. Students will demonstrate skills in spatial awareness.
4. Students will demonstrate skills in strength.
5. Students will demonstrate skills in fine motor activities (reaching, grasping, twisting, and turning).
6. Students will demonstrate skills in cleaning.
7. Students will demonstrate skills in selling (simulated).
8. Students will demonstrate skills in delivering messages and running errands.

9. Students will demonstrate skills in basic communication, basic number concepts, and arithmetic facts appropriate to their functioning level.

Intermediate Level (4-6)

Examples of job skills for intermediate level handicapped children parallel those of the primary level but are more sophisticated. Some of these are:

1. Students will demonstrate skills in gross motor activities (hopping, skipping, sit-ups, etc.).
2. Students will demonstrate skills in strength and stamina.
3. Students will demonstrate skills in gross motor coordination (lifting, carrying, pushing, pulling, etc.).
4. Students will demonstrate skills in fine motor activities (pincer grasp, screwing with screwdriver, and small parts manipulation).
5. Students will demonstrate skills in using small hand tools (hammer, hand saw, pliers, wrenches, and hand drill).
6. Students will demonstrate skills in selling (real).
7. Students will demonstrate skills in personal service jobs in the neighborhood (cleaning yards, mowing lawns, babysitting, etc.).
8. Students will demonstrate skills in basic communication, basic number concepts, and arithmetic facts appropriate to their functioning level.

SELECTED ACTIVITIES AND MATERIALS FOR ACHIEVING GOAL/OBJECTIVE STATEMENTS

Although the majority of the activities suggested in earlier chapters have emphasized cognitive and affective experiences, the activities proposed for this component of the career education model are primarily psychomotor. If ever the adage "learn by doing" were appropriate, this is the time. You may have noted that the goal statements were all expressed in terms of *skills.* Of course, some knowledge and cognitive processes are needed to communicate how to perform a skill, but they are secondary to the goal of skill performance. To be consistent with what has been said before, verbal communication about how to do things should be minimized and kept at a concrete level. Whenever possible, instructions or procedures should be demonstrated or "discovered" by pupils with guidance as needed.

There is an important distinction to be made between the activities suggested in this chapter and those presented in previous chapters. Where skills are the goals, activities are used to motivate, illustrate, or reinforce pupils in relation to their learning the skills. Goal statements expressed in terms of skills require the performance of those skills for evaluation. The activities, then, are typically successive trials at the skills themselves. For this reason, there is no need to list examples of activities, since the goals themselves specify the activities. Other means of presenting instruction in this area are discussed in Chapter 6.

Materials for Acquisition of Daily Living and Job Skills

Primary Level (K-3) .

The following examples of materials for primary level skills development are necessarily related to the cognitive aspects of performing a skill. They present visual (verbal, pictorial, human action) or auditory aids for children or instructors on "how to do it." Many of the activities lend themselves to a see-and-do or hear-and-do approach, so that instruction is not limited to the cognitive level. This is possible for most didactic materials; you have to extend the didactic level to the experiential level for best results in skill acquisition.

1. *Stories and books:*
   Arnold, D., and Posey, K. L. *Do It Yourself* (Frank E. Richards).

Barkin, C., and James, E. *What Is Money* (Children's Press, 1977).

Bethell, J. *How to Care for Your Dog* (Four Winds, 1967).

Caney, S. *Play Book* (Workman Publishing Co., 1975).

Elbert, V. F. *Easy Enameling on Metal* (Children's Press, 1975).

Frith, M., and Lerner, S. *Big Bird's Busy Book* (Random House, 1975).

Gray, G. *Keep an Eye on Kevin: Safety Begins at Home* (Children's Press, 1973).

Hintz, M., and Hintz, S. *We Can't Afford It* (Children's Press, 1977).

Johnson, H. L. *Let's Bake Bread* (Children's Press, 1973).

————. *Let's Make Jam* (Children's Press, 1975).

Klimo, J. F. *What Can I Do Today?* (Pantheon Books, 1971).

Krayer, J. *Captain Kangaroo's Whole World Catalog* (Platt and Munk, 1976).

Laird, J. *Lost in the Department Store* (Denison, 1968).

Mangi, J. *ABC Workbook* (Feminist Press, 1975).

Rinkoff, B. *No Pushing, No Ducking* (Children's Press, 1974).

Scarry, R. *Best Make-It Book Ever* (Random House, 1977).

Sharp, E. N. *Simple Machines and How They Work* (Random House, 1959).

Young, J. *Dental Health Stories* (New Readers Press).

Ziegler, S. *Something for Sara: A Beginning Book About Money* (Children's Press, 1977).

2. *Recordings (tapes, cassettes, or discs):*
   Activity Records Series (Educational Activities, Inc.). "Learning Basic Skills Through Music," "Learning Basic Skills Through Music: Health and Safety," and "Learning Basic Skills Through Music: Vocabulary"

"Basic Songs for Exceptional Children" (Concept Records). Three volumes

Ella Jenkins Record Series (Kimbo Educational). "My Street Begins at My House," and "Counting Games and Rhythms for the Little Ones, vol. 1."

"Follow Me" (American Book Co.).

Hap Palmer Record Library Series (Kimbo Educational). "Learning Basic Skills Through Music" (Green, Blue, and Red Jacket Albums), "Pretend," and "Ideas, Thoughts, and Feelings."

"Meet Mr. Mixup" (Lyons).

"Mr. Ready Health — P.E. Readiness" (Educational Projections).

Physical Fitness Recording Series (Bowman). "Music for Physical Fitness," "Fun and Fitness," and "Basic Motor and Ball Skill."

"Rhythm Record" (LeCrone Rhythm Record Company).

"Safety at Home" (EPS, Inc.).

"Shimmy Shimmy Coke-Ca-Pop" (Belwin Mills).

"The Downtown Story" (Scholastic Records).

"The Shower Song" (JoAnne Smaltz Productions).

William Janiak Record Series (Kimbo Educational). "Songs About Me," and "Developing Everyday Skills Through Movement and Songs."

3. *Films:*

"Care of Pets" (Encyclopaedia Britannica Educational Films).

"Fire Safety is Your Department" (Centron Films).

"Home Safety: It's Up to You" (Centron Films).

"Joan Avoids a Cold" (Coronet).

"The Junk Food Man" (AIMS Instructional Media Services, Inc.).

"Playground Safety — As Simple as ABC" (Centron Films).

"Primary School Bus Safety" (Centron Films).

"The Real Talking Singing Action Movie About Nutrition" (Oxford Films).

"Safety as We Play" (ACI Productions).
"Safety on the Street" (Encyclopaedia Britannica Educational Films).
"Safety with Fire" (Coronet).
"School Bus Safety and Courtesy" (Centron Films).
"Using and Caring for Art Materials" (Centron Films).
4. *Filmstrips:*
"A Visit to the Dentist" (Jim Handy Organization).
"A Visit to the Library" (Troll Associates).
"Community Helpers" (Teaching Resources Films).
"Larry Helps the Police" (Curriculum Films).
"Shopping for Groceries" (Jim Handy Organization).
"What A Doctor Sees When He Looks At You" (Troll Associates).
"What Do You Like To Do?" (Society for Visual Education).
Note: See section on multimedia kits, which includes many sound filmstrips.
5. *Television programs and videotapes:*
"Captain Kangaroo" (Columbia Broadcasting System).
"Sesame Street" (Public Broadcasting Service).
6. *Songs:*
Action Songs for Growing Up (Children's Music Center).
Bicycle Songs of Safety (Holt, Rinehart, & Winston).
7. *Toys, games, or manipulative materials:*
"Childcraft House-Cleaning Set" (Childcraft).
"Childcraft Pipe Put-Together" (Childcraft).
"Connector" (Childcraft).
"Hannibal Earns and Spends Game" (Educational Achievement Corporation).
"Inquisitive Games — Discovering How to Learn" (Science Research Associates).
"Puzzles — Senior and Deluxe Series" (The Judy Company).
Tinkertoys, Legos, Lincoln Logs, or other construction toys.
Tools (hammers, pliers, screwdrivers, and wrenches).

Arts and crafts supplies and equipment.
Cooking supplies, utensils, and appliances.
Manipulative hardware (nuts, bolts, washers, etc.).

8. *Multimedia kits:*
"Danger" (Educational Activities, Inc.). Sound filmstrip and teacher's guide.
"Dental Health Stories" (New Readers Press). Books, sound filmstrips, and teacher's guide.
"Drugs, Poisons, and Little Children" (Educational Activities, Inc.). Color sound filmstrip and teacher's guide.
"Eye and Ear Care" (Educational Activities, Inc.). Color sound filmstrip and teacher's guide.
"Health and Safety Highlights" (Scott, Foresman). Color photo charts, record album, and teacher's resource book.
Health and Safety Series (Educational Projections Corporation). Sound filmstrips, skill sheets, spirit masters and teacher's guide.
"Holidays" (Educational Projections Corporation). Sound filmstrip and transparencies.
"Keep Fit — Be Happy" (Pathescope Educational Media). Five sound filmstrips and teacher's manual.
Self Sufficiency Series (Clearvue, Inc.). Sound filmstrips and teacher's guide.
Survival Series (Clearvue, Inc.). Sound filmstrips and teacher's guide.
"What's Cooking?" (Bowmar). Posters, recipe cards, clock, cooking calendar, and teacher's guide.

9. *Miscellaneous:*
"Childsize Traffic Sign Set" (Childcraft).
"Danger" (Electronic Futures, Inc.). Flash cards and teacher's guide.
"Earning and Using Money" (David C. Cook Publishing Co.). Teaching pictures and teacher's guide.
"Things We Do and Use Around the House" (Western Publishing Co.). Transparencies.
"What We Do By Day" (National Dairy Council). Study prints.

Intermediate Level (4-6)

Skill acquisition materials for the intermediate level can be selected from most subject matter materials related to daily living or job skills. A deliberate effort should be made to ensure that the examples of daily living and job skills provided earlier in this chapter are systematically presented for handicapped children at this level. Undoubtedly, you will need to select materials independently of subject matter areas in order to present these skills. The following materials contain examples of useful resource materials.

1. *Stories and books:*
   Adams, A. H., Flowers, A., and Woods, E. E. *Reading for Survival* (Goodyear Publishing, 1978).
   Anderson, M. *Paper Mache and How to Use It* (Sterling Publishing Company, n.d.).
   Alkema, C. J. *Creative Paper Crafts in Color* (Sterling Publishing Company, n.d.).
   _____. *Masks* (Sterling Publishing Company, n.d.).
   Barkin, C., and James, E. *Managing Your Money* (Children's Press, 1977).
   _____. *Slapdash Cooking* (Lothrup, Lee, and Shepard, 1972).
   _____. *Understanding Money* (Children's Press, 1977).
   Bayles, F. *You Can Make Good Things to Eat* (Children's Press, 1975).
   Berman, M., and Shevitz, L. *I Can Make It On My Own* (Goodyear Publishing, 1978).
   Bontrogen, F. M. *Can You Give First Aid?* (New Reader's Press, n.d.).
   Cardazo, P. *The Second Whole Kids Catalog* (Bantam, 1977).
   _____. *The Whole Kids Catalog* (Bantam, 1975).
   Cobb, V. *Science Experiments You Can Eat* (J. B. Lippincott Co., n.d.).

Cooper, J. *Love At First Bite: Snacks and Mealtime Treats the Quick and Easy Way* (Alfred A. Knopf, 1977).

Freeman, D. R. *How to Read a City Map* (Children's Press, 1967).

Hautzig, E. *Cool Cooking* (Lothrup, Lee, and Shepard, 1977).

Howard, S. W. *Tin-Can Crafting* (Sterling Publishing Company, n.d.).

Ickis, M. *Weaving as a Hobby* (Sterling Publishing Company, n.d.).

Isenstein, H. *Creative Clay Work* (Sterling Publishing Company, n.d.).

Johnson, H. L. *Let's Make Soup* (Lothrup, Lee, and Shepard, 1976).

Jubara, F. *What's In The Tool Box?* (Mafex Associates, n.d.).

Klimo, J. F. *What Can I Do Today?* (Pantheon Books, 1971).

LaCroix, G. *Creating With Beads* (Sterling Publishing Company, n.d.).

Moore, E. *The Cookie Book* (Scholastic Book Services, 1973).

Newsome, A. J. *Make It With Felt* (Lothrup, Lee, and Shepard, 1972).

——— . *Spoolcraft* (Lothrup, Lee, and Shepard, 1970).

Peterson, G. *Creative Leathercraft* (Sterling Publishing Company, n.d.).

Strose, S. *Potato Printing* (Sterling Publishing Company, n.d.).

Terry, L., and Horn, D. *To Smoke or Not to Smoke* (Lothrup, Lee, and Shepard, 1969).

Weiss, P. *Scrap Wood Craft* (Lothrup, Lee, and Shepard, 1977).

Williams, B. *Pins, Picks, and Popsicle Sticks* (Holt, Rinehart, & Winston, 1977).

Yerian, C., and Yerian, M. *Creative Activities Series* (Children's Press, n.d.). *Making*, vol. 1; *Organizing*,

vol. 10; *Growing*, vol. 11; *Caring*, vol. 12; *Traveling*,
vol. 16; *Sewing*, vol. 18; and *Cooking*, vol. 19.
——— . *Fun Time Activity Books* (Children's Press,
n.d.). *Money-Making Ideas, Community Projects,
Easy Sewing Projects, Gifts for Everybody, Indoor
Gardening, Outdoor Gardens, Party Foods,* and
Working With Wood.

2. *Recordings (tapes, cassettes, or discs):*
"Drunk!" (Educational Activities, Inc.).
"Gentle, Gentle Thursday" (Bowmar Records).
"Graded Physical Fitness Exercises for Boys" (Educational Activities, Inc.).
"Graded Physical Fitness Exercises for Girls" (Educational Activities, Inc.).
"How Much Change?" (3-M Company).
"The Story of Growing Up" (Kenworthy Educational Services, Inc.). *Note:* This is directed at girls, but would also be informative for boys.
"What It Means to Grow Up" (Kenworthy Educational Services, Inc.). *Note:* This is directed at boys, but would also be informative for girls.
"Who Said It?" (Lyons).

3. *Films:*
"Art From Found Materials" (Bailey Films).
"Bicycle Safety: The Rules of the Road" (Centron Films).
"Bike-Wise-To Be Sure" (Centron Films).
"Care of Pets" (Encyclopaedia Britannica Educational Films).
"Cider Maker" (ACI Productions).
"Electrical Safety" (Centron Films).
"Home Safety: It's Up to You" (Centron Films).
"Joan Avoids a Cold" (Coronet).
"The Junk Food Man (AIMS Instructional Media Services, Inc.).
"Naturally . . . A Girl" (Personal Products).
"Playground Safety — As Simple as ABC" (Centron Films).

"Real Talking Singing Action Movie About Nutrition"
(Oxford Films).
"Safety with Fire" (Coronet).
"School Bus Safety and Courtesy" (Centron Films).

4. *Filmstrips:*
"Organizations for Children" (Educational Projections
Corp.).
Note: See section on kits for filmstrips with sound
accompaniment.

5. *Games:*
"Attribute Game" (Teaching Resources).
"The Credit Game" (Leswing Communications, Inc.).
"Monopoly" (Parker Brothers).
"Pay Day" (Parker Brothers).
"Thinklab" (Science Research Associates).
"Thinklab 2" (Science Research Associates).
"Trading Post" (Leswing Communications).

6. *Multimedia kits:*
"Coping with Menstruation" (National Center on Edu-
cation Media and Materials for the Handicapped).
Color slides, audio cassettes, transparency masters,
and teacher's manual.
"Dollars and Sense" (Educational Reading Services).
Six sound filmstrips.
"How Do You Go To School?" (Kilby Associates).
Sound filmstrip.
"How to Watch TV" (Xerox Education Publications).
Sound filmstrips and teacher's guide.
"How We Are Born" (Follett Publishing Company).
Books, charts, parent folders, and teacher's guide.
"Learning to Live Together" (Society for Visual Edu-
cation). Sound filmstrips.
"Self Care — Male Hygiene" (Interpretive Education).
Six sound filmstrips and teacher's guide.
"Utilities, Communications" (Avid Corporation). Four
sound filmstrips.
"What Happens When You Steal?" (National Center

on Educational Media and Materials for the Handicapped). Slides, audio cassettes, and teacher's manual.
7. *Miscellaneous:*
"Earning and Using Money" (David C. Cook Publishing Co.). Study prints.
"What We Do By Day" (National Dairy Council). Study prints.

REFERENCES

Bereiter, C. Elementary school: Necessity or convenience. In E. W. Eisner and E. Vallance (eds.), *Conflicting conceptions of curriculum*. Berkeley, California: McCutchan Publishing Corporation, 1974.

Brolin, D. *Programming retarded in career education*. Working Paper No. 1, University of Missouri-Columbia, September, 1974.

de Grazia, S. *Of time, work, and leisure*. Garden City, New York: Anchor Books, 1964.

Hoyt, K. B. *An introduction to career education*. Policy paper of the U.S. Office of Education, DHEW Publication No. (OE) 75-00504. Washington, D.C.: U.S. Government Printing Office, 1975.

Marland, S. P., Jr. *Career education: A proposal for reform*. New York: McGraw-Hill, 1974.

New Readers Press News. Before APL there was NRP. *New Readers Press News* 1 (1977): 1.

The Oxford English Dictionary, Volume II. London: Oxford University Press, 1961.

Wolfensberger, W. *Normalization: The principle of normalization in human services*. Toronto: National Institute on Mental Retardation, 1972.

6

IMPLEMENTING CAREER EDUCATION PROGRAMMING FOR THE HANDICAPPED

Planning and initiating career education programming for the handicapped within a school system must occur on two levels — the administrative level and the operational level. The scope of the programming model is such that successful implementation must involve both levels, although an individual teacher or counselor could initiate most elements of it with some positive benefits to children. The chances of administratively instituting the complete curriculum reform called for in this model are slim. Nevertheless, the realities of "due process" and compliance with federal and state regulations are so imposing that administrators and direct service and instructional personnel must get organized lest parents start asking questions about the individualized education plans of their children and demanding programs with appropriate content priorities.

There is already a history of professionals endorsing various educational reforms while waiting for others to push for implementation. It has long been said that "what is everybody's responsibility is nobody's responsibility." Specific responsibilities for career education programming should be fixed and all participants should know who is to do what. This chapter contains implementation guidelines for all participants. The guidelines are geared to the administrative and operational levels of both regular and special education to focus on the major administrative programming options for handicapped children in the elementary school.

In the United States innovative career education has been translated into action typically in one of three ways: as an instructional approach, as a curriculum modification, or as a combination of the two. This chapter discusses implementation in light of these three responses and provides some suggested guidelines and strategies for elementary school professionals who are responsible for programming for all children.

No matter how career education is implemented, it definitely has an impact on curriculum and should therefore be treated as a curriculum concept. The model presented in this book has incorporated the idea that career education should involve both an instructional approach and curriculum modification. Before we consider implementation approaches, we will review the basic assumptions of the model:

1. Career education for physically and mentally handicapped individuals differs significantly enough from that of the nonhandicapped that special attention must be given to curriculum development for them. This does not mean that handicapped individuals are totally unlike the nonhandicapped. Their needs are actually the same but curricular modifications must be made to guarantee that basic life career development needs are met. Because of their disabilities, learning and achievement of developmental tasks are more difficult, and specific instruction must be used. Incidental learning experienced by the nonhandicapped at home, in the community, and in children's organizations cannot be assumed in the case of handicapped children.

2. Just as there is a need for differential career education programming for the handicapped and the nonhandicapped, there is a need for some differential programming for various disability groups within the handicapped population. The individual nature of the content to be presented must be considered in order to select the best instructional approaches for that content. That is, a child with a moderate to severe hearing loss may require different content at certain points than a child with a visual handicap. For example, language development or vocabulary emphasis may be a priority for the deaf youngster while mobility and psychomotor development may be important for the blind child.

3. Formal career education programming should begin no later than the kindergarten level for any child, but for handicapped children it is extremely critical that full implementation (curriculum modification and instructional approach) begin in kindergarten. Primary instruction may not be the beginning of living and learning, but it largely influences the degree of success children will have in later experiences.

4. Neither a democratic philosophy of education nor a realistic philosophy of normalization (Wolfensberger, 1972) dictates that all children must have the same curriculum. Recent events in human rights legislation for the handicapped, which culminated in the passage of Public Law 94-142, The Education for All Handicapped Children Act of 1975, have reinforced the notion that "appropriate education" and "least restrictive alternative" are synonomous with educational programming for the nonhandicapped. Programming for the handicapped in our schools in the past has been inappropriate, and in many ways restrictive, but we cannot afford at this important time in educational history to forget that the intent and purpose of the legislation is to guarantee a free and appropriate education for individual handicapped persons. What is judged to be appropriate must be based first and foremost on *what* the individual needs to know and be able to do and, second, *how* that content can best be delivered.

5. Career education is a critical, necessary part of the educational process for handicapped children. In spite of

encouraging developments, career education is not yet a fully accepted concept in our schools. Thus, there is no guarantee that the handicapped children of this nation will receive any systematic career education programming (much less programming of the scope encouraged in this book). Educators and advocates committed to the education of the handicapped must take steps to ensure that full career education is available in all schools.

WHO IS TO IMPLEMENT CAREER EDUCATION FOR THE HANDICAPPED?

At the administrative level, implementing any type of instructional program — career education, bilingual education, consumer education, or whatever — appears to be more successful the smaller the administrative unit is. At the building level the principal maintains responsibility for administering district policies and prescribed programs and has some freedom to initiate and develop innovative programs of personal interest or concern.

Hypothetical Situation 1

Let us assume that a school district has approved of the career education concept and has endorsed the state career education plan. Further, the principals have been urged to implement the plan. (This is obviously an idealistic hypothetical situation!) Let us also assume that the district is acutely aware of the mandate of the Education for All Handicapped Children Act of 1975 (P.L. 94-142) and has made principals responsible for complying with the regulations of this law.

What is facing these principals as they attempt to meet their responsibilities? Let us bring some realism into the hypothetical situation and suggest some of the predictable obstacles each principal must surmount in this situation:

1. The majority of the teachers in the building have no real understanding of career education and probably associate it with occupational awareness. They are basically neutral to the idea and assume a unit per year on jobs or community helpers is sufficient.

2. A few of the teachers are aware of the scope of career education and will be enthusiastic advocates. About the same number will have little or no understanding of the concept of career education and will be negative to *any* program change that affects them.

3. The majority of the teachers have no real understanding of the characteristics and needs of handicapped children and generally assume that they are all mentally or educationally retarded and should expect personal and social maladjustments. They are unaware of the specifics of P.L. 94-142, but assume that they will be getting handicapped children in their classes. They have some anxieties about the situation, and they question their adequacy. They may be willing to give it a chance if they have some help.

4. A few of the teachers are aware of the intent and purpose of P.L. 94-142 and will be enthusiastic advocates for the children placed in their classes. About the same number have little or no understanding of the concept of "least restrictive alternative" or individualized programming and will be negative, perhaps even hostile, to any efforts to respond to the law.

5. A majority of the teachers come from middle-class, achievement oriented backgrounds and have had little contact with handicapped persons, with workers from occupations in the day labor, unskilled, or semiskilled categories, or with adults who have dropped out of school or were "pushed" out with few skills for coping with daily living or job demands.

6. Most of the teachers assume that their primary function is to teach basic academic skills and they believe that these skills are sufficient tools for coping with adult living.

7. A majority of the teachers are concerned with personal and social development of their pupils only insofar as those aspects of development relate to their conduct or behavior in the classroom.

8. A majority of the teachers are not fully aware of the demands that will be made of their students at the middle or junior high school level, much less the high school level, and find it difficult to relate what they are teaching at the elementary level to the stages that follow.

Although more obstacles might be in our principal's path, these will suffice for now. Keep in mind that the obstacles listed above may exist even when the career education program being considered is narrower and easier to implement than the one presented in this book. If we were to assume that the principal had read this book and the work of Brolin (1974), Cross (1974), or Gysbers and West (1975), the obstacles would increase in number because of the wider implications for curriculum content priorities.

What, then, is our principal to do? First the principal must be personally and professionally committed to the basic intents and purposes of career education and to the concept of a free and appropriate education for the handicapped. Second, the principal must approach his or her responsibility as systematically as possible. The following implementation plan suggests some of the systematic steps that should be taken:

Step 1: Develop a plan for initiating a career education program for all children in the school.
    A. Form an advisory group or task force to assist in developing the plan.
    B. Involve all teachers in developing the scope and sequence of the plan.
    C. Evaluate the current curriculum of the school to determine where changes need to be made to implement the plan.

        D.   Identify all available resources within the building faculty, the school system, and the neighborhood or school community that can support, complement, or assume responsibility for specific elements of·the plan.

Step 2:   Submit the plan to the school advisory council or Parent-Teachers' Association for reaction and input.

Step 3:   Submit the plan to school district administrative officials for approval.

Step 4:   Initiate efforts to gain the cooperation of all individuals, departments, or service components in the school system and the community that are needed to implement the program.

        A.   Appoint selected regular and special education teachers to coordinate the development of individualized educational plans for handicapped children.

        B.   Appoint selected regular and special education teachers to coordinate all contacts and cooperative efforts with others in the school system and resource persons in the community.

        C.   Develop a plan for eliciting and maintaining support from others in the school system who are advocates for career education or for the handicapped.

           (1)   Schedule visits to career education activities in the school system.

           (2)   Schedule visits to programs for the handicapped.

           (3)   Arrange for school visitations by resource persons in career education and education of the handicapped.

           (4)   Arrange for recognition of resource persons.

Step 5:   Develop a plan to elicit and maintain the cooperation and participation of all teachers on the building faculty.

        A.   Develop an in-service training plan on career education for all faculty.

      B.   Develop an in-service training plan on individualized planning and programming for the handicapped.

      C.   Establish an instructional materials collection on career education and education of the handicapped.

      D.   Establish some vehicle for communicating what is happening in career education programming to the various elementary grade levels and encourage communication between the elementary school and the middle or junior high school(s) with which it is primarily associated.

      E.   Arrange for recognition of teachers who actively involve themselves in the career education program.

Step 6: Implement the career education plan.

      A.   Employ specific strategies for accomplishing objectives in every step of the plan.

      B.   Use evaluation procedures to monitor the success of the program. (See Appendix C for sample procedures.)

      C.   Use evaluation data to modify the program.

Strategies for the Principal

1. Be an involved leader in implementing a model or plan.
2. Develop a skeleton plan or a working paper so that the advisory group has something to which it can respond.
3. Select both faculty members and parents for the advisory group. Include some who may be skeptical, or even negative, but select the majority from those who are receptive to the basic concepts of the plan to be developed.
4. Include all teachers in planning the scope and sequence of the program.

5. Set target dates for accomplishing the plan. They should be frequent enough to maintain momentum and continuity of thought, but not so frequent that planning is rushed and forced.
6. In addition to identification of available resources to assist in the plan, which may have already been accomplished for the district, identify specific resource personnel in the faculty and neighborhood community. A parent survey may be required. (See Appendix D for an example of a survey form.)
7. Select leadership people who are thoroughly committed to the plan and who are accepted by the faculty and parents.
8. Rotate leadership positions at least once a year to avoid overloads and to prevent identification of the program with an individual.
9. Use visitation to other programs as an in-service training approach.
10. Develop tangible, highly desirable means of rewarding resource personnel, and participating teachers.
11. Involve faculty in planning and conducting their own in-service training.
12. Be prompt and responsive to requests by teachers for materials and supplies related to career education activities.
13. Seek additional sources of funds for establishing the program.

Hypothetical Situation 2

Now, let us assume that a school district has not responded to the state career education plan — it has established no policies and issued no directives to the principals. The implications of P.L. 94-142 have been discussed and the potential for lawsuits from parents and the loss of federal funds for noncompliance has been considered. The principals have been directed to comply with the regulations.

Assume also that a third grade teacher in one of the elementary schools — Mrs. Doe — becomes committed to the concept of career education in its broadest sense and wants to include career education programming in her curriculum. The teacher approaches the principal and asks for approval. The principal indicates that the priority for the year is complying with the new federal law for education of the handicapped and that the building poicy is that anything that goes on in the school that may affect the handicapped must be evaluated in light of meeting the letter of the law. The principal further informs the teacher that she can anticipate one or two children who had formerly been placed in self-contained special education classes to be in the regular classroom for a majority of the school day. A summary of the school's policy for individualized educational planning is given to the teacher and she is told that whatever she decides to do, the principal would like to react to it.

What does this teacher face in attempting to follow through with the commitment to career education programming? The following obstacles are typical for any teacher in a situation like this:

1. There will be much to learn about the characteristics and instructional needs of handicapped children.
2. The type and amount of assistance she can expect from the principal, district resource persons, or building faculty is uncertain for both career education and education of the handicapped.
3. Existing elementary career education curricula are restricted largely to occupational awareness.
4. There will probably be little or no substantial effort made by the school district to purchase career education materials that are very comprehensive for the anticipated use of only one teacher.
5. There may be a tendency for administrators to place handicapped children in her class, assuming it will be the least restrictive environment and most appropriate

educational placement, even though there may not be an individual educational plan established beforehand.

6. Implementing two significant changes in instructional content and approach will require extra time and effort, especially in the first year.

In a hypothetical situation one can be as optimistic or pessimistic as necessary to make a point. Let us be rather optimistic and assume these are the only major obstacles facing this teacher. What can she do? Again, a carefully planned approach that deals systematically with the task and possible problems will be most efficient and effective. The following plan should be useful to you if you face anything like this teacher's situation:

Step 1: Develop a plan for increasing skills and level of information for children who deviate from the norm in certain learning or behavioral areas.

A. Investigate possibilities for in-service training opportunities at the local, area, or state level.

B. Contact sources such as colleges and universities, regional education service centers and intermediate school districts, or area learning resource centers to obtain readings or self-study materials designed for regular elementary teachers who have handicapped children in their classes.

C. Investigate the possibility of on-campus or extension coursework from local or area teacher education institutions.

Step 2: Develop a plan for initiating career education programming that addresses the individual needs of all children in the classroom.

A. Form a small advisory committee of parents and school personnel (principal, counselor, special education staff, school nurse, or anyone in the district with responsibility for curriculum) to assist in developing the plan.

B. Evaluate the existing curriculum and instructional

approach for the classroom to determine where changes need to be made to implement the plan.

C. Identify all available resources within the building faculty and staff, the school district, and the community (including parents) that can support, complement, or assume responsibility for specific elements of the plan.

D. Inventory all available instructional materials that can be used in the plan and determine needs for additional materials.

Step 3: Submit the plan to the building principal for reaction and input.

Step 4: Initiate efforts for eliciting and maintaining support from resource persons.

A. Schedule visits to school or community resources to verify their appropriateness and to assess the feasibility of using them.

B. Secure tentative agreements to assist in the programming planned.

C. Arrange for recognition of resource persons.

Step 5: Implement the career education plan.

A. Employ specific strategies for accomplishing objectives in every step of the plan.

B. Use evaluation procedures to monitor the success of the program. (See Appendix C for an example procedure.)

C. Use evaluation data to modify the program.

Strategies for the Regular Classroom Teacher

1. Increasing skills and level of knowledge of the handicapped takes time. Set short-term and long-term goals for competencies needed now and in the future.

2. Develop a skeleton plan or working draft of a program so that the advisory committee has something to which it can respond.

3. Select advisory committee members from among the most supportive school staff available and from a cross-section of parents. Be sure parents of handicapped children do not dominate to the extent that goals are circumvented.
4. Set target dates for accomplishing the plan but be realistic in terms of how much can be changed.
5. Evaluate existing curriculum and instructional approaches with a focus on content areas covered, skill areas covered, and the range and frequency of use of instructional activities or methods.
6. Based on data from the curriculum evaluation, decide how delivery will be made for each of the content areas identified as priority areas. That is, decide whether instruction should be delivered through a comprehensive separate subject matter curriculum, through infusion or integration into the existing curriculum, or a combination of both.

Hypothetical Situation 3

For our third hypothetical situation we will depict a group of professionals who want to ensure that handicapped children in their programs receive comprehensive career education. Let us assume that a special class teacher (or a resource room teacher who has control of curriculum content) has become convinced that career education really can be a workable approach to meet the major developmental tasks of the children. The school district has no local career education plan or policy. The special class teacher, Mr. Levy, has experimented with some of the concepts and skills associated with career education for some time, but now wants to be more systematic and comprehensive. He asks for a meeting with the principal and the director of special education and makes a request to proceed in this direction. They remind him that there is no specified curriculum for children in self-contained classrooms, although they assume that the primary focus should continue to be basic academic skills and social development. Whatever the teacher wants to do is all right with them if the parents have no objections and the children still have some basic instruction in reading, arithmetic, and writing. They also remind the teacher that it is likely that some children will be out of the classroom for part of each day in a resource room. (In the case of a resource room teacher, children would be in regular classes part of the day). This means losing control over curriculum for some students for portions of the day.

What obvious obstacles will face this teacher? The following problems would be fairly typical:

1. The kind and amount of support the principal and the director of special education are likely to provide is minimal.
2. Curriculum modifications will be left up to the teacher almost exclusively.
3. A well-developed sequential curriculum for handicapped children that includes a comprehensive coverage of career education does not exist.
4. A commitment to the notion of a comprehensive approach to career education does not provide the teacher with instant experience and knowledge of career development desirable for curriculum development and instruction. There will be much to learn.
5. There will probably be few, if any, appropriate career education materials available for the students, and probably no substantial effort will be made by the school district to purchase such materials.
6. During the first few years of compliance with P.L. 94-142, administrators are likely to be more concerned with the social aspects of placement of handicapped children in considering the "least restrictive environment" than with the appropriate curricular needs related to total developmental needs for present and future living.
7. Making curriculum modifications in an instructional program that has been primarily focused on academic

skill development will take time, effort, and commitment. It may take two years to establish a consistent philosophy, make priority decisions on curriculum content, and modify instructional techniques.

What can a teacher do in this type of situation? As in the first two hypothetical situations, the obstacles are not going to disappear with the wave of a magic wand or with a systematic plan. It will take a high level of commitment to the needs of children *and* a systematic approach to eventually accomplish the change. The model and strategies that follow are parallel to the suggestions outlined for the regular classroom teacher in Hypothetical Situation 2 above:

Step 1: Develop a plan for increasing knowledge and experience in career development, adult adjustment, and the world of work.
  A. Investigate possibilities for in-service training opportunities at the local, area, or state level.
  B. Contact sources such as colleges and universities, regional education service centers and intermediate school districts, or special career education projects to obtain readings or self-study materials on career education.
  C. Investigate the possibilities of on-campus or extension coursework from local or area teacher education institutions.

Step 2: Develop a plan for initiating a career education based curriculum.
  A. Form a small advisory committee of parents and school personnel to assist in developing the plan.
  B. Evaluate the existing curriculum and instructional approach for the classroom or resource room to determine where changes need to be made to implement the plan.
  C. Identify all available resources within the building faculty and staff, the school district, and the community (including parents) that can support,

complement, or assume responsibility for specific elements of the plan.

D. Inventory all available instructional materials that can be used in the plan and determine needs for additional materials.

Step 3: Submit the plan to the building principal and the director of special education.

Step 4: Initiate efforts for eliciting and maintaining support from resource persons.

A. Schedule visits to school or community resources to verify their appropriateness and to assess the feasibility of using them.

B. Secure tentative agreements to assist in the programming planned.

C. Arrange for recognition of resource persons.

Step 5: Implement the career education plan.

A. Employ specific strategies for accomplishing objectives in every step of the plan.

B. Use evaluation procedures to monitor the success of the program. (See Appendix C for a sample procedure.)

C. Use evaluation data to modify the program.

Strategies for the Special Class or Resource Room Teacher

1. Set short-term and long-term goals for obtaining more knowledge and skill in the areas of career education, career development, adult adjustment, and the world of work.

2. Develop a skeleton plan or working draft of an ideal program so that the advisory committee has something to which it can respond.

3. Select advisory committee members from among the parents most actively involved in the community and the most supportive school staff.

4. Identification of resource persons is a critical step and can mean the difference between a "paper" program and an operational program.

5. Evaluate existing curriculum and instructional approaches with a focus on content areas covered, skill areas covered, and the range and frequency of instructional activities or methods.

6. Based on data from the curriculum evaluation, decide how delivery of the prioritized content and skill areas will be handled.

7. To ensure that students are placed in "least restrictive environments" and get an *appropriate* curriculum, the teacher (or some child advocate) should evaluate the content and instructional approaches of those environments. This can be a delicate procedure in terms of professional relationships, and must be conducted objectively and diplomatically, with the needs of the children always in mind.

The Elementary School Guidance Counselor

A fourth professional can be involved in implementing a comprehensive career education model at the building level: the elementary school guidance counselor. Not all elementary schools have the services of a counselor, but for those that do, a word needs to be said about his or her role. Given the broad perspective of our career education model for the elementary level handicapped child, special attention should be focused on the following service areas.

Values, Attitudes, and Habits

It is obvious that there is a relationship between values, attitudes, and habits and the role of the counselor, for counselors frequently must deal with concerns in these areas. Counselor involvement can take several forms, the most obvious being individual or small group counseling. There are many guidance materials that can encourage and assist children in looking at their values, valuing, and attitudes. The counselor might design a program to increase understanding of self, for example, and either coordinate materials and activities for teachers or team-teach with teachers in a teaching unit.

Human Relationships

Counselors may do individual and group counseling of students to help them learn to relate better with others. Counselors may also consult with teachers and parents to help students improve their relationships with others, or they might be involved in coordinating special materials or activities with teachers.

Occupational Information

Traditionally, counselors have been involved in the collection and dissemination of occupational information. Currently, however, occupational information is being defined more broadly than occupational awareness, and includes such issues as realities of the world of work, volunteerism, occupational stereotyping, and the process of occupational choice. Any of these issues may provide opportunities for counselors to design and conduct in-service workshops for teachers; special events days for a class, grade level, or school; or guidance groups for students.

Acquisition of Actual Job and Daily Living Skills

It may be that counselors of elementary children will think it somewhat more difficult to be involved in the area of actual skill acquisition. However, if acquisition of actual job skills is considered in its broadest sense, it includes a number of skills that a counselor is prepared to deal with. Acquisition of academic skills to aid in job or daily living demands would be the most common involvement. Counselors should be available to talk to handicapped students as they begin to confront realities such as limited academic achievement and disabilities that interfere with skill acquisition. Further, counselors should be ready to assist in teaching certain coping or survival skills at school or in the community, like the use of resource persons and special information centers. Academic, prevocational, and community living competencies must be established as strongly as possible during the elementary school years, and a counselor will find much to do in working with children who fail to acquire those skills or who resist or refuse to acquire them for various reasons.

BASIC PEDAGOGICAL ISSUES IN IMPLEMENTING CAREER EDUCATION PROGRAMMING

The most frequent pedagogical approach of advocates of career education has been an insistence that new concepts and skills should be infused or integrated into the traditional structure of the curriculum. This approach not only attempts to accomplish a major goal of career education — *to make subject matter more relevant* — but it also attempts to ameliorate concerns of traditional educators who fear that career education will displace them or negate their traditional status. While career education has been defined primarily as occupational awareness, this approach has worked relatively well at the elementary level. There has been no problem incorporating various concepts and skills in social studies and language arts areas to make career education (occupational awareness) a visible component of the school program.

The model presented in this book, and the basic assumptions of Brolin (1974), Cross (1974), and Gysbers and West (1975), expand the definition of career education to the point that it is much more comprehensive than occupational awareness. The immediate implication for delivery of this model challenges the traditional approach. Some of the issues were pointed out in the strategies for teachers in the preceding section. At this point I would like to discuss some of the advantages and disadvantages of the three major alternatives for delivery: infusion, separate programming, or a combination of infusion and separate programming.

Infusion

Some of the possible advantages of infusing a comprehensive career education model for the handicapped into a traditional curriculum are:

1. Infusion makes abstract academic content more concrete, more relevant, and consequently, easier to learn.
2. Infusion increases the possibility for exposure to a wider range of career education concepts and skills.
3. Infusion assumes that everyone in the educational process will be participating from his or her own perspective, providing a broad-based support system.
4. If infusion is operative in the entire educational program, there is some assurance that the content of the curricula in regular classes will be more appropriate for many handicapped children.

Some of the possible disadvantages of the infusion approach in delivering a comprehensive model of career education for the handicapped are:

1. Infusion tends to take an "activities" approach. This means that career education activities are used to enhance the learning of concepts and skills of a basic subject matter area. The concepts and skills of the activities related to career education are left to incidental learning.
2. Infusion does not lend itself to achievement evaluation for the types or level of learning desired for career education concepts or skills, because evaluation tends to focus on the subject matter concepts and skills.

3. Infusion does not encourage, or in many cases *permit*, repetition of career development concepts and skills that are needed by many handicapped children for overlearning.
4. Infusion is not systematic enough to ensure that the scope and sequence of the desired concepts and skills will be covered.
5. Infusion depends upon the willingness and ability of teachers to incorporate the concepts and skills of a comprehensive model into each of the basic academic skill areas. In essence, it is a voluntary commitment unless the school district or building principal requires it, monitors it, and provides support in doing it through in-service training, materials, resources, etc.

Separate Programming

Delivering career education through separate programming can be accomplished in three basic ways: (a) a total school curriculum in which career education represents the curriculum focus and all subject matter concepts and skills are infused into this thematic framework — very much like the occupational core curriculum conceptualized by Hungerford (1941) and developed by DeProspo and Hungerford (1946); (b) a separate subject matter area, like science, health, or music; and (c) a unit teaching approach where discrete objectives are taught during specific times set aside from basic academic instruction.

There are some distinct possible advantages for separate programming of a comprehensive career education model for the handicapped. Gibson (1972) cited the following:

1. Separate programming assures that concentrated attention will be given at some time during the year to the goals and objectives for career education at a given level.
2. Separate programming communicates to pupils the importance of career development.

161

3. Separate programming may make more of an impact and lead to more effective and efficient learning through focused learning.
4. Separate programming offers students an opportunity to "tie together" the various career development concepts and skills they have been exposed to over a period of time.
5. Separate programming can serve as a motivating technique for upcoming basic subject matter content and experiences.
6. Separate programming provides a specific opportunity to take better advantage of the expertise of the elementary school counselor through using him or her as a resource person, a team teacher of a unit, or a consultant to individual pupils.
7. Separate programming may facilitate the undertaking of special activities and the extensive use of community resources.

As persuasive as these advantages for separate programming are, there are also some significant disadvantages. They include:

1. Separate programming adds to an already crowded, highly competitive curricular marketplace.
2. Separate programming leads to specialization, which may require an instructor with special training in the area. Subject matter programming eventually leads to certification regulations.
3. Separate programming as a curriculum or subject matter course is difficult to implement without a well-developed, systematic, sequential curriculum guide or a published curriculum series. Neither of these currently exists.
4. Separate programming of career education concepts and skills in a total curriculum or subject matter format requires some standardized achievement assessment instruments to evaluate the functioning level of students

and provide data for effectiveness of instruction. These do not presently exist.

5. Separate programming of certain components may lead to artificiality of instruction. That is, there are certain content areas related to actual job or daily living skills that logically belong in basic subject matter instruction. Certain aspects of consumer education, for example, should be taught in math and social studies; certain aspects of human sexuality and body care should be taught in science or health; and, obviously, such critical job and daily living skills as reading, writing, spelling, and arithmetic should be taught separately at the elementary level.

6. Separate programming could become a type of tokenism to satisfy the advocates of career education while effectively keeping the academic areas "pure" by avoiding infusion.

Combination of Infusion and Separate Programming

As in many things in life, a compromise between extreme positions is frequently the happiest solution. In a sense, the use of both infusion and some type of separate programming results in the best of both worlds. The advantages of such an approach include:

1. A combination of infusion and some separate programming permits a balance between teaching critical academic skills (with career education content incorporated for application) and critical career education concepts and skills (with basic skills incorporated as problem-solving tools or aids to making certain job or daily living demands go easier).

2. A combination approach avoids, to some extent, the issue of adding to an overcrowded curriculum and poses less of a threat to subject matter specialists.

163

3. Combining the two approaches permits the teacher to be involved in the total education process by retaining responsibility for covering all critical areas, but without having to personally take on certain instructional goals.

4. Infusion and separate programming combined provide a unique opportunity to tie together concepts and skills learned in both academic and career education instruction.

5. A combination of infusion and separate programming provides the handicapped pupil in the regular classroom with the critical elements necessary for a "responsive environment," rather than a restrictive environment.

Although there are some potential disadvantages of a combination approach, the major disadvantage is that there is no way to control the infusion aspect. A school district or building principal can prescribe certain teaching units to be taught separately and which can be monitored effectively. Infusion can be urged or encouraged, but there is no really effective way of determining whether it has been done appropriately or at all. The issue rests completely with each teacher's commitment to career education and confidence in using the many instructional activities that are effective for infusing career development content and skills into basic academic subjects.

It is my belief that infusion alone is not sufficient for coverage of career education objectives at the elementary level. Neither is separate programming, in the form of total curriculum or as a separate subject. The current dearth of well-developed curricula and assessment instruments precludes the advisability of using separate programming except under experimental conditions. Assuming there were curricula, assessment instruments, and trained teachers, factors such as differences between grade levels, degree of handicapping conditions, and instructional setting would still have a bearing on how career education content should be delivered. Figure 6.1 outlines some possible delivery approaches.

	Mildly Handicapped		Moderately to Severely Handicapped	
	K-3	4-6	K-3	4-6
Regular Class or Resource Room	Infusion and Unit Teaching	Infusion and Unit Teaching	Infusion and Separate Subject*	Infusion and Separate Subject*
Special Class	Infusion and Separate Subject	Infusion and Separate Subject	Total Curriculum	Total Curriculum

*Moderately or severely handicapped students in regular grades or resource rooms will most likely be visually handicapped, auditorially handicapped, or learning disabled.

Figure 6.1. Recommended approaches for delivery of career education instruction based on grade level, degree of handicap, and instructional setting.

MAJOR INSTRUCTIONAL ACTIVITIES FOR INFUSION OR UNIT TEACHING OF CAREER EDUCATION CONTENT

As stated above, a teacher's confidence in using the many instructional activities that are effective in teaching career education concepts and skills is critical. For that reason, I would like to review the major instructional activities recommended in previous chapters. The readers of this book undoubtedly possess a wide range of educational and professional experience. For some of you, this section may be unnecessary; for others, it may provide a useful review or even new information in the context of teaching career education content. The instructional activities include field trips; use of resource persons; use of audio-visual materials; use of toys, games, puppets, and manipulative materials; role playing, simulation, construction, and problem solving.

Field Trips

There is no doubt that field trips are more fun for children than for teachers, but you can have fun, too, if your field trips are carefully planned. Gibson (1972, pp. 50-51) has presented an excellent checklist for teachers or counselors in planning:

Checklist for Field Trip Planning

Bertram Kiley Elementary School

I. Teacher Preparation

_____ Administrative consent
_____ Permission from the site
_____ Parental permissions
_____ Transportation (and parking) arrangements
_____ Rest stop provisions
_____ Meal arrangements (if needed)
_____ Provisions for pupils not participating
_____ First aid provisions
_____ Emergency arrangements
_____ Coordination with other faculty
_____ Other _____

II. Classroom Preparation

_____ Objectives identified and explained to pupils
_____ Pupils participate in planning
_____ Site representatives participate in planning
_____ Class discussions held
_____ Guides or maps prepared
_____ Observation checklists prepared
_____ Appropriate reading and written assignments made
_____ Field trip "rules" explained
_____ Other _____

III. Plans for Follow-up

_____ Follow-through discussions planned
_____ Follow-through assignments made
_____ Evaluation
_____ Letters of appreciation to personnel of site visited
_____ Other _____

Note: It is not anticipated that every item will be checked for every field trip. It is suggested that as each item is accomplished, a checkmark be placed in the blank provided. For each item that is inappropriate, place a zero in the blank provided.

The primary responsibility for planning a field trip rests with you. This responsibility can be shared or delegated, but you are the one who will answer for any problems. Planning can be shared with pupils, parent volunteers, community volunteers, or paraprofessionals. If planning and arrangements are delegated, you must take the time and effort to train the person or persons involved in good planning techniques. The checklist above would be a good tool for any planning assistant.

Most important, perhaps, is deciding exactly *why* a field trip is needed. The best field trips involve a limited set of objectives that are completely understood by the teacher, any delegated assistant, the pupils, and the person(s) at the field trip site who assisted in the arrangements. This usually requires a lot of good communication. It starts with a clear understanding of the concept(s) you want to teach and a decision that a field trip would be the most effective activity.

Use of Resource Persons

Having resource persons come to your class or school is a good alternative to a field trip; it certainly avoids some of the problems of planning and conducting field trips. The two

167

activities have something in common, however. They both depend on the effective contribution of someone else. As such, they can turn out to be "tricks" or "treats."

The most common types of classroom visitors are parents or community workers who come in and talk about their work. Current books on career education restrict most, if not all, discussion of "outsiders" to these types of resource persons. The comprehensive model of career education proposed in this book opens up countless other possibilities. Resource persons for the areas of attitudes, values, and habits or human relationships may not be needed as frequently as those who provide occupational information, but the general need for actual job or daily living skills makes the scope of the visitor program virtually limitless.

The secret to success in using guest speakers with elementary children is to select someone you *know* has the ability to communicate his or her expertise to your group. This requires some effort on your part to screen individuals sufficiently before inviting anyone to visit your class. Once you have made an invitation, you can increase your chances for a successful session by providing the person with as much specific information as possible concerning *what* you want the children to learn, *why* they need this information, and *how* they respond best. Your speaker will need to know how long the children can listen, whether or not demonstrations are appropriate (if so, specific suggestions should be included), and how children need to be able to ask questions to clarify and organize the information they receive. (See Appendix E for a sample letter to a potential speaker.)

Use of Audio-visual Materials

It has been said that if a firsthand observation or experience is not possible or feasible, a secondary experience through visual or auditory media can accomplish some, if not all, of the same objectives. The effectiveness of learning from television programs such as "Sesame Street," "The Electric Company," "Zoom," "Mister Rogers' Neighborhood," and others is acknowledged by most educators. Teachers do not need to be sold on the effectiveness of good films, filmstrips, videotapes, recordings, or multimedia kits; they have been traditional teaching aids for years. What, then, needs to be said about using audio-visual materials?

The primary concern in using such materials is that they aid in teaching precisely what you want them to teach. That is, is the content valid? We say that we want our tests to be valid and test what we want to test, *all* of what we want to test, and *nothing* but what we want to test. We are not always so strict with instructional materials; we are perhaps too easily satisfied if the materials are generally related to the topic of concern and, most importantly, if they keep the pupils occupied. To be fair, however, it is not necessarily appropriate to apply the same validity standards to materials and to tests. It is a bonus if materials contain good information that goes beyond the specific content desired but, often, materials do not have all of what we want covered in exactly the way we would like it covered.

The critical factors in determining whether materials are valid or not for your purposes are (a) do they match the objectives you have set and (b) do they avoid any negative learning? It is important to screen out audio-visual materials that contain subtle stereotyping of the handicapped, minority groups, or women. Misinformation may also be imparted if some of the material is obsolete. Both of these problems are especially likely to appear in older films. Previewing possible materials means that you may order films or recordings and end up returning them unused. That is time-consuming and expensive, but it *is* necessary.

An important resource to know about for making the most of materials that relate to your objectives and meeting the needs of your students, particularly those with hearing or auditory perception problems, is Media Services and Captioned Films. These two groups have fine mailing lists of available audio-visual materials. (See the Publisher/Distributor List at the end of the book for the addresses.)

169

Use of Toys, Games, and Manipulative Materials

Toys, games, and manipulative materials can be used very effectively with young children generally, and with many handicapped children, if used purposefully. Some teachers dismiss these items as "frivolous" or as "time-fillers" at best. Others see them as concrete experiences that teach certain concepts or skills better than other activities. The issue, again, is one of validity for your purposes. If you are planning a unit on playing cooperatively and your objective is to demonstrate the social skills of sharing, taking turns, and being a good winner or loser, an appropriate game would be a much better activity than a film, an individual activity assignment, or some seatwork. The same game might be used on another (or on the same) occasion to teach specific concepts or skills related to consumer education, history, or literature.

You will find toys, games, and manipulative materials worthwhile if you remember these simple guidelines:

1. Choose your items strictly on the basis of their appropriateness for your objectives.
2. Items should be simple to operate and easily understood by children.
3. Carefully plan procedures for directing, supervising, observing, and evaluating the outcome(s) of the activity.

Puppetry

The use of puppets for teaching career education concepts and skills may seem to fall into the same category as toys, games, and manipulative materials. It is presented separately because puppets should be seen primarily as teacher-directed rather than pupil-oriented stimulus materials. This is not to say that pupils never manipulate the puppets; it means that whenever they are used the teacher must be directing or monitoring the activity to provide the structure for specific learning.

The use of puppets is frequently seen as a "gimmick," but there are some techniques teachers can practice to prevent the novelty from becoming mere gimmickry. Terryl M. Asla, professional puppeteer and director of the University of Kansas Puppet Program, has suggested the following guidelines (Asla, 1977):

1. Choose an environment for presenting the puppet that fits the size of the group involved. A quiet place with a minimum of visual and auditory distractions works best.

2. As puppeteer, situate yourself behind a screen that is placed on a low table. Put your chair behind the screen and the children's chairs directly opposite you on the other side of the table. The puppet should be slightly above the eye level of the seated children.

3. Purchase screens or make them from cardboard boxes. It is helpful to have a small hole about three inches in diameter in the middle of the puppet screen so that you can observe the children. The hole can be covered with white netting, surgical gauze, or a piece of nylon hosiery to prevent the children from looking through or being distracted.

4. Use puppets that fit your objectives. Some puppets depict human characteristics but are asexual and non-racial; others show sex and racial characteristics. Some are animals, and some are Muppet-like characters that have both human and animal characteristics. Whatever your choice, a puppet should have a discernable personality, even before you put it on, that fits your objectives.

5. Select puppets about 14 inches tall, with bright colors and textures and faces about the size of your hand. Smaller puppets are good for children to play with, but for your manipulation and teaching, the larger ones seem to attract and hold the attention of children better. The puppets should have at least two movements, such as movement in space, ability to twist the neck, movement of the head, or movement of the mouth.

6. Learn a few basic skills to manipulate puppets, including:

   A. *Eye contact.* Learn to direct the puppet's gaze unerringly at any person or object so there is no doubt where the puppet is looking.
   B. *Listening movements.* Learn the movements of leaning the body forward and cocking the head to show the puppet is listening.
   C. *Reacting cues.* Learn the following movements to show the children the puppet understands what they are saying or thinking: nodding the head (agreement), opening the mouth (awe), shaking the head (in agreement), quivering (excitement, anticipation), and patting the screen edge rapidly (excitement).
   D. *Responding cues.* Learn the following movements to reinforce something the children have said or done: rearing back (surprise, unbelief, "wow" reaction), falling down (shock), pounding on the screen edge ("It's too much" or "I can't stand it" reaction).
   E. *Mouth synchronization.* Learn the following movements to give the puppet credibility as the *real* person talking: *closed position* is used when the puppet comes to the end of an idea or sentence cluster; *closed to mid-open position* is used when the puppet is talking, particularly on words beginning with b, p, m, f, v, and w; *wide open posiiton* is used primarily for exclamations ending in a vowel, like "No!," "Yea!," and "Oh!"

7. Make the puppet's voice different from your normal speaking voice, but this doesn't mean that your voice must be high and squeaky. It should be clear and understandable and it should not hurt your throat. It works best to elongate words and cut down on the pauses between words. You should practice the delivery until

it feels natural and there is no danger of slipping in and out of it while the puppet is "talking."

Puppetry is not a traditional instructional activity and teachers rarely receive any specific instructions on techniques. It does take some "ham" — the ability to lose yourself in the activity — but remember, you are behind a screen and young children make a responsive audience. Try it, and keep it up, even if the first few experiences are less than what you would like.

Role Playing

Role playing (or sociodrama as it is more accurately called) in the classroom is meant to be an educational experience, not a form of therapy. Through it, children can explore, experience, develop concepts and skills, and acquire social learning that they might otherwise be denied in their own, more limited roles as pupils, sons or daughters, and brothers or sisters. They can witness and experience consequences of behaviors that they might never attempt outside such safe surroundings.

When a group role plays in an unrehearsed and spontaneous manner, a sociodrama is being played out. The purpose of this experience is the solution or resolution of some common problem. With elementary children, the problems to be resolved will ordinarily not be overly serious. You can opt for role playing whenever the typical concerns of an age group emerge or when some critical incident occurs that poses a new situation and, thus, a problem for them to solve. This approach is typically associated with personal or social problems (attitudes, values, habits, and human relationships), but there is no reason why it cannot be used for job or daily living skill problems.

Ordinarily you decide what activity fits your objectives best and proceed to implement it. In the case of role playing, it has been suggested that one of the prerequisites for using it is that most of the group must want or feel the need for exploring the situation in this way (Hoover, 1964). If your pupils have never experienced role playing before, your introduction of it

173

may be critical for its later effectiveness. The following guide-lines are based on Garrison's (no date) suggestions for role playing as a teaching technique:

1. *Setting and Props.* Some children find it easier to identify with a role if you give them a single simple stage prop. A collection of hats, caps, and dime store eyeglasses will fit most of your needs.

2. *Getting Started.* You should begin by discussing common problems related to whatever concepts or skills are to be taught. Discussion stimulates spontaneity in the actual role play that follows. Children who are accustomed to a rigid, structured classroom atmosphere will require more preparatory discussion.

3. *Selecting a Theme.* Select a common problem that has meaning for most of the children. It can concern relationships with peers, teachers, or parents, or relate to a performance skill required at school, at home, or in the community.

4. *Warm-up Period.* You can get the children "warmed up" by asking a series of questions related to the problem to be resolved. Accept all answers or statements from the children, but use your questions to stimulate thinking about alternatives and factors to be considered. Questions such as "What would happen if . . .?" "What would you do if . . . ?" or "What is another way to try . . . ?" are good for this.

5. *Describing the Situation.* You must describe the situation in very clear and understandable terms. Do not give any solutions or dictate what direction the play should take or how long it should last. Keep it simple.

6. *Selection of Participants.* Participation should be voluntary, but you should be on the alert for a child who should be encouraged to step in and assume a new role.

7. *Duration of Role Play.* The more you use this technique, the more adept you will become in sensing when a situation has been "milked dry." At times you

might want to stop a role play before a solution or conclusion is reached and turn it into a class discussion with questions like "What do you think will happen next?" or "What will John do?" The duration of the role play should be based primarily on how effective the activity is — it may range from a matter of seconds to ten or fifteen minutes.

8. *Role of Teacher or Counselor.* As the "director," you must enter into the spirit of the play and, for younger or more immature children, model roles from time to time. When the dialogue bogs down, you will probably have to ask questions like "Now, what would he do?" or shift to another player and ask, "What happens now?" to keep things going.

9. *Atmosphere.* You have to make the children feel that although the problem is real, their part in it now is "just pretend." They should feel free to play any role without fear of criticism for their role playing ability or of the decisions, solutions, or feelings that emerge.

10. *Evaluation.* You may evaluate the activity by reacting to the entire dramatization with a question like, "What did you think of it?" It is typical to get responses such as, "It's fun," or "Edwin wasn't a very good principal." These responses should be treated casually, but try to get enough feedback to get a feel for what they think of the activity and how it might be improved. A more critical evaluation of a role playing session focuses on the concept or skill that was specified in your objective for the class. You will probably want to question the children to find out whether they feel a solution to the problem emerged. If the children disagree or are ambivalent, you may want to re-enact the situation with the same or different participants to see if it can be more conclusive or produce another alternative.

Role playing has not been widely used in the elementary school because of the time and emphasis placed on academic skills over personal and social skills. Our comprehensive model of career education calls for new emphases and, thus, some new techniques; give this one a try.

Simulation

Simulation activities have been used in elementary schools to some degree for years. A mini-grocery store set up in the corner of a classroom is the classic example of an attempt to create all the appearances of reality without having the complete reality. This type of activity is ordinarily used to provide experiences with some learned concepts or skills. There is only so much pupils can learn through listening, observing, or reading. Actual performance of the skill or application of the knowledge is the ultimate test of acquired learning. Simulation is not only a teaching technique, but also an evaluation technique.

Simulated situations can be set up for a number of career education objectives at the primary level. If you are trying to teach grooming, a simulated bath or dressing area could be set up with mirror, combs, and brushes. Pupil-made accessories can make it look "homey." If you wish to teach simple, basic food preparation for breakfast or snacks, a mini-kitchen could be arranged. A styrofoam cooler set on end makes a nifty refrigerator, and a countertop and sink complete the scene. (A hot plate really tops it off!) You have limitless possibilities for teaching various occupational awareness concepts: With creative use of two or three dividers, corners can become official looking, mini-sized health clinics, libraries, stores, banks, offices, cleaners, repair shops, or whatever.

Simulation for the intermediate level along the same lines is possible, but usually requires more semblance of reality. Harrison (1973) has described one of the most complex simulation classroom systems to appear in educational literature. He created a micro-economy for a sixth grade class based on realistic principles of capitalism, social values, personal values, self reliance, and responsibility for personal behavior. Although this approach has merit, it is not recommended for every teacher and you should not feel compelled to use such an elaborate simulation. There *are* other ways.

Probably the most traditional simulation in the classroom is the creation of a series of jobs or work roles, with students assigned on some rotating basis. You will not have a true simulation unless there is some reality in the procedures used in "hiring," "supervising," "quality control," "paying," or "firing." The extent to which you use this simulation approach depends upon your objectives. Work assignments are appropriate tools, but they may not actually be simulations.

Hoyt, Pinson, Laramore, and Mangum (1973) suggest a more sophisticated approach to simulated work experience that appeals to intermediate level students. Their "product outcome" technique centers on a simulated "company" formed by the students. With this approach you help the students think of ideas for a product or service they would like to produce or offer, aid in the selection of one of these, direct the management-worker system needed, assign or direct the selection of students for the various work roles, and supervise the production, advertisement, and sale of the goods or services. Examples of products that have been produced in projects of this type include puzzles, wall plaques, artificial flower arrangements, note pads, doll clothes, silk screened posters and cards, and games of all types. Simulated companies might provide such services as cleaning, babysitting, errand running, plant sitting, snow shoveling, or yard work. In either type of project, the students can learn a variety of concepts and skills that cut across all the major components of a comprehensive career education model.

Construction

"Constructional activity" refers to the process of building, forming, or fashioning a three-dimensional object or series of such objects (Miller and Boyd, 1970, p. 7). Perhaps you have more frequently heard the terms "handcrafts," "arts and crafts," or "creative arts" in reference to constructional activities. Because these terms have a negative connotation for some people and there is a somewhat stereotyped view of educational programming for the handicapped stemming from misuse or overuse of arts and crafts activities, there is a movement to use the term "industrial arts" instead. The basic elements of industrial arts (tools, materials, and processes) are certainly the basic elements of constructional activity, so there is no reason to reject this term if, in fact, your constructional activity is not art or craftwork for objectives relating to aesthetics.

The basic assumption for using constructional activities at the elementary level is that children who have selected or been assigned tasks that are significant to them will seek information, develop skills in measurement, organization, problem-solving, and using tools, to gain a background necessary to make or produce the desired object. If the handicapped children for whom you are responsible are in a regular class or a curriculum that is fairly restrictive in terms of separate programming options, constructional activity is most effective as a technique in unit teaching. The activity concept is not dependent upon acceptance of the unit method, however. For example, in science an activity can be used to promote understanding of the principles of electricity; in arithmetic an activity can strengthen number concepts; in social studies an activity can illustrate the importance of the invention of some machine or device; and in music a constructional activity can allow students to experience rhythm instruments.

Before selecting constructional activity as the technique you want to use in teaching a unit or infusing certain concepts or skills into subject matter areas, ask yourself the following questions:

1. Does the constructional activity have a direct relationship to other experiences in the unit?
2. Are the handicapped children I am concerned about ready for the activity in terms of background and skill in construction?
3. Does this activity meet a need that is significant to the handicapped children in my class?

4. Will this activity contribute to a better understanding of the concepts of this unit or the academic concept being taught?
5. Will this activity promote critical thinking, cooperative planning, and problem-solving skills?
6. Is this activity practical in terms of available time, tools, and materials?
7. Is this activity more effective than other experiences that can be used?

Problem Solving

As children play, study, or work together, certain difficulties are bound to arise that slow down or block their progress. These difficulties or problems have to be solved or resolved before their lives can proceed smoothly. Those who learn how to solve their problems during the childhood years continue to solve them as adults. Those whose problems were solved by parents or teachers, or worse yet, who never had problems identified as external, solvable problems, grow up to be adults who have difficulty in solving their own problems or seeing any hope in trying.

Your choice of problem solving as a teaching technique should be based on real or simulated problems that are of interest to the children. It might involve a personal or social problem that centers on a "what if" situation with several alternative solutions that have predictable consequences. It might involve an improvement problem of a product, a situation, or an environment. It might also involve a remediation problem — "Why isn't this working?" or "What could you do to make this work again?"

Problem solving is frequently associated with the inquiry method of learning and is thought to be ideal for individual learning experiences at a learning center. This may be true for gifted or talented children or for those who are independent learners, but it is not appropriate for children who are mentally handicapped or who do not have the skills to go through a problem-solving situation alone. You will need to provide personal direction in this activity, for the class, for a small group, or for the individual. You should guide students through the problem-solving process in a step-by-step approach that includes the following steps:

1. Careful observation and analysis of the situation leading to an accurate identification of the problem.
2. Suggestions of possible solution(s) to the problem.
3. Objective and thorough consideration of available information related to the causes of the problem and the feasibility of the solution(s).
4. Tentative selection of the best alternative(s) based on the available knowledge.
5. Experimentation or trial of the selected alternative.
6. Evaluation and acceptance of the alternative tried, or readjustment in light of new evidence or changes in the problem situation.

CONCLUSION

Regardless of how carefully you plan and attempt to follow some of the suggestions from this book or your own creative instincts, some things will go wrong. You will feel alone and outnumbered at times; you will feel discouraged and defeated at times. It would be an injustice to you and gross dishonesty to say any less. If you are prepared for this possibility, however, it might not be too overwhelming. Further, if some simple cautions are kept in mind, you may avoid some of the problems that can affect your working with handicapped students.

First, do not give up when your first or even second effort at some technique or approach does not work. Give yourself a fair chance to grow and to develop the skills you want and need to accomplish your goals. Too frequently methods, techniques, or materials are rejected prematurely at the first signs of difficulty or non-success. Remember that with assistance or more experience, you will be more likely to make it work.

Second, do not let activities become ends in themselves.

We all fall into this trap when an activity works effectively the first time and becomes a routine approach. After a while the reason for using that activity in the first place is forgotten or becomes less obvious.

Third, avoid attachment to materials. This is not currently as big a temptation as it may be when more materials become available. Whether it be a filmstrip series, a five year supply of carpet samples that just *has* to be used, or certain spirit masters, few resources deserve to be valued in themselves without reference to specific needs of individuals. When materials take over, purpose and intent go by the boards.

Fourth, avoid attachment to processes. Every school has teachers whose teaching practices are so routine it can set its calendar (if not its clocks) by them. Mrs. G's class always has plant projects, Miss L's class always makes Christmas ornaments, Mr. B's class always records and charts the temperatures for February, etc. To keep devotion to processes from getting out of hand, a good rule of thumb is to demand that every process used in the past be justified over other possible processes each year. During a time when "zero based budgeting" is seen as an efficient technique, zero based curriculum development should also be given a try.

Fifth, you should be careful to avoid becoming enamored of constructional activity products. Some teachers (and professionals who work with the adult handicapped) become so preoccupied with the end product of learning or training that they lose sight of the reason for producing the object at the outset. Products are important only in passing and should be a symbol or reflection of a learning process that was used to accomplish something far more person-oriented than the object itself.

Finally, you should avoid becoming too attached to the model of career education for the handicapped presented in this book. It is only a rough map of the frontiers of career education for young handicapped children and, like all early maps, it should yield to more sophisticated, comprehensive guides. As this model was an attempt to move from the traditional, so might it be considered traditional some day. Do not let it become a closed system.

Toffler (1971) joined other critics of American education who are concerned about closed systems and traditionalism when he stated:

> The present curriculum and its division into airtight compartments is not based on any well thought out conception of contemporary needs. Still less it is based on any grasp of the future, any understanding of what skills Johnny will require to live in the hurricane's eye of change. (p. 412)

We may be uncomfortable with, and even resentful of, noneducators telling us that we are on the wrong track, but I am firmly convinced that Toffler and others who are concerned about *what* we are teaching our youth are absolutely correct. Curriculum reform must and will occur — in regular education and in special education. With more and more children with disabilities that affect their development having access to all of education, it is essential for advocates for the handicapped to be a part of that reform. Perhaps *you* can be in the thick of it.

REFERENCES

Asla, T. M. *Getting kids to talk with puppets: A puppet methodology for evoking spontaneous language samples from children.* Unpublished manuscript, Department of Speech and Drama, University of Kansas, Lawrence, Fall, 1977.

Brolin, D. *Programming retarded in career education.* Working Paper No. 1, University of Missouri-Columbia, September, 1974.

Cross, F. R. *Elementary school careers education: A humanistic model.* Columbus, Ohio: Charles E. Merrill Publishing Company, 1974.

DeProspo, C. J., and Hungerford, R. H. A complete social program for the mentally retarded. *American Journal of Mental Deficiency* 51 (1946): 115-122.

Garrison, I. *Socio-drama — as a teaching technique.* Unpublished manuscript, no date.

Gibson, R. L. *Career development in the elementary school.* Columbus, Ohio: Charles E. Merrill Publishing Company, 1972.

Gysbers, N. C., and West, L. L. *Career education: Its implications for the educable retarded.* Working Paper No. 3, University of Missouri-Columbia, March, 1975.

Harrison, A. E. *How to teach children twice as much.* New Rochelle, New Jersey: Arlington House, 1973.

Hoover, K. *Learning and teaching in the secondary school.* Boston: Allyn & Bacon, Inc., 1964.

Hoyt, K. B., Pinson, N. M., Laramore, D., and Mangum, G. L. *Career education and the elementary school teacher.* Salt Lake City, Utah: Olympus Publishing Company, 1973.

Hungerford, R. H. The Detroit plan for the occupational education of the mentally retarded. *American Journal of Mental Deficiency* 46 (1941): 102-108.

Miller, W. R., and Boyd, G. *Teaching elementary industrial arts.* South Holland, Illinois: The Goodheart-Willcox Company, Inc., 1970.

Toffler, A. *Future shock.* New York: Bantam Books, 1971.

Wolfensberger, W. *Normalization: The principle of normalization in human services.* Toronto: National Institute on Mental Retardation, 1972.

APPENDIX A

HOME WORKER'S CHECKLIST; CLASSROOM WORKER'S CHECKLIST

Career Education for the Handicapped Child

HOME WORKER'S CHECKLIST*

Dear Parent: Please place a checkmark beside each item your son or daughter accomplishes satisfactorily for each day of the week beginning Monday.

	M	T	W	T	F
1. Gets up on time					
2. Makes bed					
3. Straightens room or area					
4. On time for meals					
5. Washes hands and face before meals					
6. Brushes teeth after meals					
7. Helps with housework					
8. Is considerate of others					
9. Is dependable					
10. Goes to bed on time					

Comments:

Please ask _____ to bring this form with him

on _____ . Thanks for your help.
(date due)

_____
Teacher

*Modified form from R. L. Gibson, *Career Development in the Elementary School* (Columbus, Ohio: Charles E. Merrill, 1972).

CLASSROOM WORKER'S CHECKLIST

Student	Work Week Dates				
	M	T	W	T	F
1. On time to school					
2. Keeps desk/locker neat					
3. Uses classroom equipment and supplies appropriately					
4. Accomplishes assigned tasks					
5. Sees things that need to be done and responds					
6. Follows directions					
7. Takes pride in effort					
8. Relates well to others					
9. Relates well to authority figures					
10. Is dependable					

APPENDIX B
JOB CLUSTERS

Clustering is an attempt to organize the 25,000 jobs in the United States into a manageable, understandable system. The attached fifteen clusters, although not containing all jobs, are a means of relaying the wide scope of careers available in any one interest area. Within each cluster are careers that require a variety of skills and training.

1. **Personal Services**

   Rationale: Careers which supply specific services that are purchased or obtained to fulfill a particular need or desire of a person.

   Beautician
   Shoe Repairman
   Social Worker
   Insurance Agent
   Refrigeration, Air
       Conditioning and
       Heating Mechanic
   TV Repairman
   Radio Repairman

   Babysitter
   Priest
   Missionary
   Furniture Upholsterer
   Barber
   Cleaner and Laundry
       Manager
   Telephone Operator
   Minister

Rabbi   Mortician
Tailor

2. **Health Services**

Rationale: Careers related to the determination of health problems, physical caring for the problems and exploring possible preventive measures.

Psychologist   Optometrist
Doctor   Pharmacist
Orderly   Podiatrist
Practical Nurse   Laundry and Sterilizer
Occupational Therapist   Osteopath
Medical Secretary   Psychiatrist
  and Librarian   Nurse
Veterinarian   X-Ray Technician
Dentist   Nurse's Aide
Laboratory Technician   Hospital Administrator
Chiropractor   Dental Technician
Anesthesiologist   Dental Hygienist
Speech Pathologist   Bacteriologist

3. **Construction**

Rationale: Careers related to building.

Mobile Home Builder   Surveyor
Architect   Paperhanger
Plumber   Pipefitter
Plasterer   Engineer
Mason   Draftsman
Bricklayer   Carpenter
Printer   Electrician
Industrial Designer   Excavator
Cabinet Worker   Cement Mason
Roofer   Heavy Equipment
                                  Operator

4. **Manufacturing**

   Rationale: Careers which create a product.

Machine Operator	Industrial Designer
Machine Maintenance	Sheet Metal Worker
Electronic Engineer	Skilled Tradesman
Assembly Line Operator	Tool and Die Operator
Mobile Home Assembler	Chemist
Welder	Mechanical Engineer
Industrial Traffic Manager	

5. **Transportation**

   Rationale: Careers related to the movement of people and things and improvement of or care for the necessary equipment.

Truck Driver	Brakeman
Pilot	Locomotive Engineer
Body and Fender	Service Station Manager
Repairman	and Attendant
Traffic Control Manager	Auto Mechanic
— Airlines	Bus and Taxi Driver
Aerospace Engineer	Conductor
Station Agent	

6. **Agri-Business and Natural Resources**

   Rationale: Careers related to the productive use of land.

Farmer	Poultryman
Dairyman	Petroleum Engineer
Feed Store Manager	Rancher
Miner	Butcher
Soil Conservationist	Farm Equipment
Agricultural Engineer	Salesperson
Agronomist	Farm Agent

Petroleum and Natural
Gas Production Worker
Farm Manager

Fish and Game Manager
Mining Engineer
Wildlife Manager

7. **Public Service**

Rationale: Careers which provide a service for individuals, some of which are tax supportive.

Kindergarten-Elementary
Teacher
State Policeman
Janitor
Certified Public
Accountant
School Administrator
Food and Drug Inspector
Court Recorder
Fireman
Urban Planner
City Policeman
Nursery School Teacher

Lawyer
Counselor — School,
Employment,
Rehabilitation
Refuse Collector
Junior and Senior
High Teacher
Government Service
Civil Engineer
Librarian
Court Bailiff
Military
Probation Officer

8. **Environment**

Rationale: Careers related to the protection, improvement of and proper use for the surroundings that influence a life.

Forest Ranger
Gardener
Landscape Architect
Camp Counselor
Fish and Game Warden
Horticulturist
Park Ranger
Tree Surgeon
Geophysicist

Range Manager
Recycling Operator
Naturalist
Meteorologist
Biologist
Forestry Aide
Geologist
Environmental Engineer

9. **Hospitality and Recreation**

Rationale: Careers which enhance leisure for mankind.

Stewardess	Waiter
Restaurant Manager	Short Order Cook
Social Director	Steward
Waitress	Cook
Restaurant Hostess	Chef
Travel Agent	Golf Pro
Dietician	Cashier
Swimming Pool Manager	Baker
Hotel-Motel Manager	Athlete

10. **Fine Arts and Humanities**

Rationale: Careers related to the cultural and aesthetic improvement of human life.

Professional Musician	Cartoonist
Dancer	Singer
Author	Playwright
Literary Writer	Music Arranger
Music Critic	Fashion Designer
Art Critic	Commercial Artist
Actress	Music Teacher
Conductor	Poet
Sign Painter	Piano Technician
Music Director	Radio and TV Director
Stage Designer	Actor
Composer	Film Editor
Orchestra Leader	Jeweler
Free-lance Artist	Singing Teacher
Floral Designer	Orchestrator
Sculptor	

11. Communications and Media

Rationale: Careers related to the transmission of information.

Journalist	Radio-TV Announcer
Technical Writer	Electronic Technician
Audio-control Technician	Lighting Technician
Proofreader	Foreign Correspondent
Staff Programmer	Sportscaster
Sound Engineer	Maintenance Technician
Script Writer	Reporter
Newswriter	Transmitter Technician
Photoengraver	Printer
Photographer	Video Technician
Lecturer	

12. Marketing and Distribution

Rationale: Careers which facilitate the development and economic movement of a product.

Salesman	Consumer Product Seller
Statisticians	Systems Analyst
Packaging and Designer	Sales Engineer
Marketing Researcher	Economist
Production and Control	Sales Supervisor
Position	Wholesale and Retail
	Distributor

13. Marine Science

Rationale: Careers related to the understanding, exploration and commercial uses of the sea.

Marine Biologist	Physicist
Seaman	Aquatic Biologist
Commercial Fisherman	Marine Geologist
Geophysicist	

14. Business/Office

Rationale: Careers related to the efficient management of the business community.

Office Manager	Trailer Salesman
Personnel Director	Bank Teller
Advertising Worker	Receptionist
Data Processor	Stenographer
Computer Operator	Computer Programmer
Public Relations Worker	Bookkeeper
Accountant	Key Punch Operator
Secretary	Purchasing Agent
File Clerk	Bank Management

15. Consumer and Homemaking Education

Rationale: Careers related to the purchase and proper use of products for the home.

Interior Decorator	Drapery Maker
Appliance Demonstrator	Credit Interviewer
Home Demonstration Agent	Seamstress
Price Control Agent	Fashion Coordinator
Milliner	Model
Homemaker	Extension Agent
Nutritionist	Home Economist

APPENDIX C

CAREER EDUCATION PROGRAMMING EVALUATION CHECKLIST

	Yes	No
1. The objectives of the career education program are stated and understood by		
a. faculty	___	___
b. guidance staff	___	___
c. administration	___	___
d. parents	___	___
2. These objectives are consistent with		
a. the overall educational objectives of the building unit	___	___
b. the overall educational objectives of the district	___	___
c. the general objectives of the school guidance program	___	___
d. the general objectives of the school special education program	___	___

3. There is a written plan for achieving the school's career education program objectives.   ____ ____

4. The planning of this program cooperatively involved
    a. faculty   ____ ____
    b. parents   ____ ____
    c. community personnel   ____ ____
    d. school resource specialists   ____ ____

5. The operation of the program itself involves
    a. faculty   ____ ____
    b. guidance personnel   ____ ____
    c. community resource personnel   ____ ____

6. The career education program makes provisions for pupils to
    a. develop values, attitudes, and habits   ____ ____
    b. develop human relationships   ____ ____
    c. expand occupational information   ____ ____
    d. acquire job skills   ____ ____
    e. acquire daily living skills   ____ ____

7. The experiences provided for pupils include
    a. observation of work and workers   ____ ____
    b. simulation or actual work experiences   ____ ____
    c. identification and practice of good work habits   ____ ____
    d. integration of career development concepts with subject matter instruction   ____ ____
    e. separate programming for career development concepts when appropriate   ____ ____
    f. individualized experiences resulting from individualized educational plans   ____ ____

8. The career education program makes
   provision for
   a. team teaching   ___ | ___
   b. cooperative planning   ___ | ___
   c. curriculum development   ___ | ___
   d. materials acquisition   ___ | ___
   e. assessment of community resources   ___ | ___
   f. parent communication system   ___ | ___

9. The career education program is
   evaluated at least annually   ___ | ___

10. The evaluation involves input from
    a. faculty   ___ | ___
    b. pupils   ___ | ___
    c. parents   ___ | ___
    d. guidance staff   ___ | ___
    e. special education staff/consultants   ___ | ___
    f. community resource personnel   ___ | ___

11. The results of evaluation are used for
    program planning and improvement   ___ | ___

12. The achievements and activities of
    the program are reported regularly to
    a. school district administrators   ___ | ___
    b. faculty   ___ | ___
    c. parents   ___ | ___
    d. community resource personnel   ___ | ___
    e. community at large   ___ | ___

APPENDIX D

SAMPLE
PARENT SURVEY
LETTER

Dear Parent:

    As a member of _____ Community, you are important to us in many ways -- too many to list them all. But one is the fact that you can help us direct our young people toward a better understanding of the world of work.

    In our elementary school, we are interested in exploring many areas of work and daily living. The best way to learn about this is to ask the one who knows the most -- the parent. I would appreciate very much if you would fill out the following information about yourself and have your child return it to me.

    1) Occupation:

    2) Would you like to talk to a class about your job or hobby? Yes _____ No _____

    3) Would you be able to take time from your job and come to school during the school day? Yes _____ No _____

    4) Is your work or interest related to math, reading, or writing? (That is, can we show how these subjects are used in your work?) Yes _____ No _____

    5) Could your work or interest be related to daily living skills? Yes _____ No _____

    6) Would you object to being video taped? Yes _____ No _____

If you have any questions, please feel free to call me at __(phone)__ between 3:00 and 3:30 p.m.

    I appreciate your taking time to answer these questions. If your answer to Item 2 is "yes," you may hear from me in the near future. Thanks.

APPENDIX E

SAMPLE LETTER TO POTENTIAL GUEST SPEAKER

Thank you very much for your willingness to participate in our program. Without your cooperation, this phase of our program could not exist.

The objective of these sessions is not to get students to make career choices, but, rather, to help students realize that everyone works and that all useful work is honorable. We hope to acquaint them with the wide variety of occupations that exist and to make their present schooling more relevant to their futures. There are many things to become other than cowboys, firemen, nurses, and teachers!

First Steps: Planning a Career Development Activity in Your Classroom (DeKalb, Illinois; Northern Illinois University, Revised August, 1972).

Your company or business may have some materials it would furnish for you to bring along — perhaps some pamphlets. You might check with your public relations office. Please bring your tools or whatever you work with. Certainly, if you wear a uniform or special clothing of any kind (welding hood?), bring or wear it if you can. Here are the kinds of things we would like to hear about:

What is your job title or description?

Briefly describe what you do.

What aptitudes or skills are important for your job?

Do you have to deal with the public? If so, would you care to comment on this?

If you are separated from people most of the time, working with *things,* how do you feel about that?

Do you prefer *not* having to deal with the public or fellow workers?

What do you consider the best points of your job? The worst?

Is your job personally rewarding and fulfilling? Do you enjoy going to work? Do you recommend it as one of the alternatives students should consider?

You may want to touch upon the financial aspect. Do you consider the pay to be adequate, very good, unsatisfactory?

What is the outlook? Will this type of employment exist when these students enter the world of work?

What changes in equipment, automation, personnel, training requirements have you experienced in the time you have been in this field?

What training is required? (High school? Trade school? College? Apprenticeship? Graduate degrees?)

Is the field difficult to enter? (Union membership, professional school entrance quotas, etc.)

How does this type of career relate to what these students do now in school?

General information on working conditions, bosses, employees, etc.

APPENDIX F

PUBLISHER/ DISTRIBUTOR LIST

ACI Productions
35 W. 45th Street
Eleventh Floor
New York, New York 10036

Advanced Learning Concepts,
   Inc.
211 W. Wisconsin Avenue
New York, New York 10016

Agency for Instructional
   Television
National Instructional
   Television Center
Box A
11 W. 17th Street
Bloomington, Indiana 47401

AIMS Instructional Media
   Services, Inc.
626 Justin Avenue
Glendale, California 91201

Allyn & Bacon, Inc.
470 Atlantic Avenue
Boston, Massachusetts 02210

American Book Company
450 W. 33rd Street
New York, New York 10001

American Guidance Service,
   Inc.
Publishers Bldg.
Circle Pines, Minnesota 55014

Argus Communications
7440 Natchez Avenue
Niles, Illinois 60648

Arista Records
1776 Broadway
New York, New York 10019

Aspect IV Educational Materials
Co.
14 Glenwood Avenue, Box 2087
Raleigh, North Carolina 27602

Atheneum Publishers
122 E. 42nd Street
New York, New York 10017

Audio-Visual Instructional
Devices
20-24 Little Neck Blvd.
Bayside, New York 11360

Avid Corporation
Instructional Systems Division
Ten Tripps Lane
East Providence, Rhode Island
02914

Bailey Films
6509 De Longpre Avenue
Hollywood, California 90028

Bantam Books, Inc.
666 Fifth Avenue
New York, New York 10019

Gerald Beasley
600 West 48th Street, S.
Wichita, Kansas 67217

Behavioral Publications, Inc.
Human Sciences Press
72 Fifth Avenue
New York, New York 10011

Belwin-Mills
16 W. 61st Street
New York, New York 10023

Benziger, Bruce, & Glencoe, Inc.
17337 Ventura Blvd.
Encino, California 91316

BFA Educational Media
2211 Michigan Avenue
Santa Monica, California 90404

Bowmar Publishing
Corporation
4563 Colorado Blvd.
Los Angeles, California 90039

Bowmar Records
622 Rodier Drive
Glendale, California 91201

Bradbury Press
2 Overhill Road
Scarsdale, New York 10583

Centron Educational Films
1621 West 9th
Lawrence, Kansas 66044

Changing Times Education
Service
1729 H Street, N.W.
Washington, D.C. 20006

Childcraft Education
  Corporation
20 Kilmer Road
Edison, New Jersey 08817

Children's Book and Music
  Center
5373 West Pico Blvd.
Los Angeles, California 90019

Children's Press, Inc.
1224 W. Van Buren Street
Chicago, Illinois 60607

Chronicle Guidance
  Publications
Moravia, New York 13118

Churchill Films
662 N. Robertson Blvd.
Los Angeles, California 90069

Clearvue Inc.
6666 N. Oliphant Avenue
Chicago, Illinois 60631

Columbia Broadcasting System
  Television Network
CBS, Inc.
51 W. 52nd Street
New York, New York 10019

Concept Records
P.O. Box 524
New York, New York 11710

David C. Cook Publishing
  Company
850 N. Grove Avenue
Elgin, Illinois 60120

Coronet Instructional Films
Coronet Building
65 E. South Water Street
Chicago, Illinois 60601

Counselor Films, Inc.
1728 Cherry Street
Philadelphia, Pennsylvania
  19103

Criterion Books, Inc.
6 West 57th Street
New York, New York 10019

Curriculum Films, Inc.
10 E. 40th Street
New York, New York 10016

Curriculum Innovations, Inc.
Highwood, Illinois 60040

Curtis Audio-Visual Materials
165 W. 46th Street
New York, New York 10036

Dell Publishing Co., Inc.
1 Dag Hammarskjold Plaza
245 E. 47th Street
New York, New York 10017

T. S. Denison and Company, Inc.
5100 W. 82nd Street
Minneapolis, Minnesota 55437

Denoyer-Geppert Company
Subsidiary of Times Mirror
  Company
5235 Ravenswood Avenue
Chicago, Illinois 60640

207

Dodd, Mead & Company
79 Madison Avenue
New York, New York 10016

Doubleday & Company, Inc.
245 Park Avenue
New York, New York 10017

Doubleday Multimedia
Box C-19518
1371 Reynolds
Irvine, California 92713

E. P. Dutton & Company, Inc.
201 Park Avenue S.
New York, New York 10003

Education Service Center
Region XIII
6504 Tracor Lane
Austin, Texas 78721

Educational Achievement
Corporation
P.O. Box 7310
Waco, Texas 76710

Educational Activities, Inc.
Box 392
Freeport, New York 11520

Educational Dimensions
Box 146
Great Neck, New York 11023

Educational Design Associates
P.O. Box 915
East Lansing, Michigan 48823

Educational Projections
Company
3070 Lake Terrace
Glenview, Illinois 60025

Educational Reading Service
Division of Troll Associates
Mahwah, New Jersey 07430

Educational Research Council
of America
Rockefeller Bldg.
Cleveland, Ohio 44113

Electronic Futures, Inc.
57 Dodge Avenue
New Haven, Connecticut 06473

Encyclopaedia Britannica, Inc.
425 N. Michigan Avenue
Chicago, Illinois 60610

EPS, Inc.
2304 East Johnson
Jonesboro, Arkansas 72401

Extension Media Center
University of California
2223 Fulton Street
Berkeley, California 94720

Eye Gate House, Inc.
146-01 Archer Avenue
Jamaica, New York 11435

Family Communications, Inc.
4802 Fifth Avenue
Pittsburgh, Pennsylvania 15213

Farrar, Straus, & Giroux, Inc.
19 Union Square, W.
New York, New York 10003

Feminist Press
SUNY/College at Old Westbury
Box 334
Old Westbury, New York 11568

Field Educational Publications
2400 Hanover Street
Palo Alto, California 94304

Folkways Records and Service
Corporation
43 W. 61st Street
New York, New York 10023

Follett Publishing Company
1010 W. Washington Blvd.
Chicago, Illinois 60607

Four Winds Press
Box 126
Bristol, Florida 32321

General Learning Corporation
250 James Street
Morristown, New Jersey 07960

Ginn & Company
191 Spring Street
Lexington, Massachusetts 02173

Goals, Inc.
499 Arapaho Central
Richardson, Texas 75080

Golden Press, Inc.
850 Third Avenue
New York, New York 10022

Goldshall Design Associates,
Inc.
420 Frontage Road
Northfield, Illinois 60093

Goodyear Publishing Co., Inc.
1640 Fifth Street
P.O. Box 2113
Santa Monica, California 90401

Grosset & Dunlap, Inc.
51 Madison Avenue
New York, New York 10010

Guidance Associates
757 Third Avenue
New York, New York 10017

E. M. Hale & Company
128 W. River Street
Chippewa Falls, Wisconsin
54729

Hallmark Card, Inc.
25th & McGee Streets
Kansas City, Missouri 64141

Harcourt Brace Jovanovich, Inc.
757 Third Avenue
New York, New York 10017

Harper & Row Publishers, Inc.
10 E. 53rd Street
New York, New York 10022

Holiday House, Inc.
18 E. 53rd Street
New York, New York 10022

Holt, Rinehart & Winston
383 Madison Avenue
New York, New York 10017

Houghton Mifflin Company
2 Park Street
Boston, Massachusetts 02107

Human Development Training
  Institute
7574 University Avenue
La Mesa, California 92041

Imperial Instructional Tapes,
Special Education Material, Inc.
484 S. Broadway
Yonkers, New York 10705

Instructo Corporation
Cedar Hollow & Matthews Road
Paoli, Pennsylvania 19301

International Marketing
  Corporation
P.O. Box 790
Norman, Oklahoma 73069

Interpretive Education
P.O. Box 2341
Kalamazoo, Michigan 49001

Jalmar Press, Inc.
391 Munro Street
Sacramento, California 95825

Jim Handy, Inc.
2861 East Grand Blvd.
Detroit, Michigan 48211

Judy Company
310 N. 2nd Street
Minneapolis, Minnesota 55401

Kenworthy Educational Service,
  Inc.
P.O. Box 3031
Buffalo, New York 14205

Kilby Associates
P.O. Box 1113
Pendleton, Oregon 97801

Kimbo Educational
P.O. Box 477
Long Branch, New Jersey 07740

King Features
235 East 45th Street
New York, New York 10017

Alfred A. Knopf, Inc.
201 E. 50th Street
New York, New York 10022

Knowledge Aid
6633 W. Howard Street
Niles, Illinois 60648

LeCrone Rhythm Record
  Company
819 N.W. 92nd Street
Oklahoma City, Oklahoma
  73120

Lerner Publications Company
241 First Avenue, N.
Minneapolis, Minnesota 55401

Leswing Communications, Inc.
750 Adrian Way
San Rafael, California 94903

Leswing Press
750 Adrian Way
San Rafael, California 94903

Listener Educational
Enterprises, Inc.
6777 Hollywood Blvd.
Hollywood, California 90028

Lothrop, Lee & Shepard
Company
105 Madison Avenue
New York, New York 10016

Lyons
530 Riverview Avenue
Elkhart, Indiana 46514

3-M Company
3130 Lexington Parkway, S.
St. Paul, Minnesota 55121

Macmillan Company
866 Third Avenue
New York, New York 10022

Mafex Associates, Inc.
90 Cherry Street
Johnstown, Pennsylvania 15902

McGraw-Hill
1221 Avenue of the Americas
New York, New York 10020

McGraw-Hill Films
1221 Avenue of the Americas
New York, New York 10020

McKnight Publishing Company
P.O. Box 2854
Bloomington, Illinois 61701

Media Services and Captioned
Film
U.S. Department of HEW
330 Independence Avenue, S.W.
Washington, D.C. 20201

Melmont Publishers
Division of Children's Press
1224 W. Van Buren Street
Chicago, Illinois 60607

Charles E. Merrill Publishing
Company
1300 Alum Creek Drive
Columbus, Ohio 43216

Milton Bradley Company
Springfield,
Massachusetts 01101

Mini Productions, Inc.
192 Hyeholde Drive
Corapolis, Pennsylvania 15108

William Morrow & Company,
Inc.
105 Madison Avenue
New York, New York 10016

Motivation Records
Argosy Music Corporation
Mamaroneck, New York 10543

Ms. Foundation for Women
370 Lexington Avenue
New York, New York 10017

National Broadcasting
   Company, Inc.
30 Rockefeller Plaza
New York, New York 10019

National Center on Educational
   Media and Materials for the
   Handicapped
The Ohio State University
220 West 12th Avenue
Columbus, Ohio 43210

National Dairy Council
Chicago, Illinois 60606

National Instructional
   Television Center
Box A
11 W. 17th Street
Bloomington, Indiana 47401

New Dimensions in Education,
   Inc.
160 Dupont Street
Plainview, New York 11803

Henk Newenhouse
Division of NOVO
1825 Willow Road
Northfield, Illinois 60093

New Readers Press
Division of Laubach Literary,
   Inc.
P.O. Box 131
Syracuse, New York 13210

New York State Board of
   Education
99 Washington Avenue
Albany, New York 12210

OIDMA, Ltd.
P.O. Box 3868
Centerdale, Rhode Island 02911

Oxford Films, Inc.
1136 N. Las Palmas Avenue
Hollywood, California 90038

Pantheon Books, Inc.
22 East 51st Street
New York, New York 10022

Parker Brothers
Division of General Mills
Fun-Group, Inc.
Salem, Massachusetts 01970

Pathescope Educational Films,
   Inc.
71 Weyman Avenue
New Rochelle, New York 10802

Pennant Educational Materials
4680 Alvarado Canyon Road
San Diego, California 92120

Personal Products Company
Education Department
Milltown, New Jersey 08850

Pitman Publishing Corporation
6 Davis Drive
Belmont, California 94002

Platt & Munk Publishers
Division of Questor Educational
  Products
1055 Bronx River Avenue
Bronx, New York 10472

Popular Science Audio-Visuals
5235 Ravenswood Avenue
Chicago, Illinois 60640

Public Broadcasting Service
15 W. 51st Street
New York, New York 10019

G. P. Putnam's Sons
200 Madison Avenue
New York, New York 10016

Raintree Publishers, Ltd.
205 W. Highland Avenue
Milwaukee, Wisconsin 53203

Random House, Inc.
201 East 50th Street
New York, New York 10022

Frank E. Richards Publishing
  Company, Inc.
330 First Street
Box 370
Liverpool, New York 13088

Roberts Audio-Visual Learning
  Arts
123 South Hillside
Wichita, Kansas 67211

Scholastic Book Services
Division of Scholastic Magazines
50 W. 44th Street
New York, New York 10036

Scholastic Kindle Filmstrips
904 Sylvan Avenue
Englewood Cliffs
New Jersey 07632

School Specialty Supply, Inc.
212-218 South Santa Fe
Salina, Kansas 67401

Science Research Associates
259 East Erie Street
Chicago, Illinois 60611

Scott Education Division
104 Lower Westfield Road
Holyoke, Massachusetts 01040

Scott (William R.), Inc.
8 West 13th Street
New York, New York 10011

Scott, Foresman & Company
1900 E. Lake Avenue
Glenview, Illinois 60025

Charles Scribner's Sons
597 Fifth Avenue
New York, New York 10017

Shawnee Press, Inc.
Delaware Water Gap,
Pennsylvania 18327

Silver Burdett Company
250 James Street
Morristown, New Jersey 07960

JoAnne Smaltz Productions
Parsons, Kansas 67357

Society for Visual Education
1345 Diversey Parkway
Chicago, Illinois 60614

Steck-Vaughn Company
P.O. Box 2028
Austin, Texas 78767

Sterling Publising Company,
Inc.
2 Park Avenue
New York, New York 10016

Teaching Resources
Corporation
100 Boylston Street
Boston, Massachusetts 02116

Teaching Resources Films
New York Times
Station Plaza
Bedford Hills, New York 10507

TOT-PAC
391 Munroe Street
Sacramento, California 95825

Troll Associates
320 Rte. 17
Mahwah, New Jersey 07430

The Ungame Company
P.O. Box 964
Garden Grove, California 92642

Valiant Instructional Materials
Corporation
237 Washington Avenue
Hackensack, New Jersey 07602

Value Communications, Inc.
Value Tales
P.O. Box 1012
La Jolla, California 92308

Vanguard Press, Inc.
424 Madison Avenue
New York, New York 10017

Viking Press, Inc.
625 Madison Avenue
New York, New York 10022

Vocational Films
111 Euclid Avenue
Park Ridge, Illinois 60068

Henry Z. Walck, Inc.
750 Third Avenue
New York, New York 10017

Walker & Company
720 Fifth Avenue
New York, New York 10019

Franklin Watts, Inc.
730 Fifth Avenue
New York, New York 10019

Western Publishing Company,
Inc.
850 Third Avenue
New York, New York 10022

Westinghouse Learning
Corporation
Department AAP
100 Park Avenue
New York, New York 10017

Albert Whitman & Company
560 W. Lake Street
Chicago, Illinois 60606

H. Wilson Corporation
555 West Taft Drive
South Holland, Illinois 60473

Workman Publishing Company,
Inc.
231 E. 51st Street
New York, New York 10022

Xerox Education Publications
A Xerox Publishing Company
245 Long Hill Road
Middletown, Connecticut 06457

Young People's Records
Children's Record Guild
100 6th Avenue
New York, New York 10013